PEOPLE SKILLS

Guiding you to Effective Interpersonal Behaviour

Bill Sultmann & Tony Burton

AUSTRALIAN ACADEMIC PRESS

First published 2003 by
Australian Academic Press
32 Jeays Street
Bowen Hills QLD 4006
Australia
www.australianacademicpress.com.au

@ Copyright 2003 Bill Sultmann and Tony Burton

Copying for Educational Purposes
The Australian Copyright Act 1968 (Act) allows a maximum of one chapter or 10% of this book, whichever is the greater, to be copied by any educational institution for its educational purposes provided that the educational institution (or the body that administers it) has given a remuneration notice to Copyright Agency Limited (CAL) under the Act.

For details of the CAL licence for educational institutions contact CAL,
19/157 Liverpool Street, Sydney, NSW 2000. E-mail info@copyright.com.au

Copying for Other Purposes
Except as permitted under the Act, for example a fair dealing for the purposes of study, research, criticism or review, no part of this book may be reproduced, stored in a retrieval system, or transmitted in any form or by any means electronic, mechanical, photocopying, recording or otherwise without prior written permission of the publisher.

National Library of Australia Cataloguing-in-Publication data:

Sultman, W. F.
People skills: guiding you to effective interpersonal behaviour

Bibliography.
ISBN 1 875378 48 0.

1. Interpersonal relations. 2. Interpersonal communication.
I. Burton, A. M. (Anthony Miles), 1948- . II. Title.

158.2

Cover, illustration and text design by Ingrid van Grysen of Australian Academic Press, Brisbane. The illustration represents how our perceptions influence our behaviours; what we see, hear and say are all affected by our perceptions of the world.

Typeset in Palatino by Australian Academic Press, Brisbane.
www.australianacademicpress.com.au

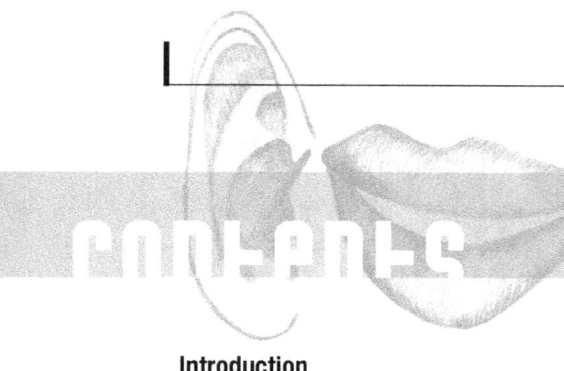

Contents

	Introduction	1
Chapter 1	**Thinking About People Skills**	3
Chapter 2	**Functioning in the Real World: A Framework for Interpersonal Development**	10
Chapter 3	**How "I" Function: The Effective Self**	20
Chapter 4	**How "we" Function: Relationship Development Skills**	36
Chapter 5	**How "Groups" Function: Group Process Development**	49
Chapter 6	**Thriving in Organisations: Contributing to Effective Workplaces**	64
Chapter 7	**Everyone is a Leader: Facilitating Interpersonal Development**	80
Chapter 8	**Keeping on, Keeping on: Sustaining Interpersonal Development Through Renewal**	95
Chapter 9	**Putting it all Together**	106
	Bibliography	109

About the Authors

Bill Sultmann

Bill Sultmann is the newly appointed Executive Director (Edmund Rice Education) in Saint Francis Xavier Province of the Christian Brothers. Before accepting this position, Bill was the Director of the Catholic Education Office in the Diocese of Toowoomba.

A registered teacher and psychologist, Bill's professional experiences have included teaching (primary, secondary, tertiary), guidance consultancy and administrative roles in Catholic and government sectors. He holds bachelor's degrees in arts and educational studies, master's degrees in educational psychology and Christian leadership, and a research doctorate in educational psychology. Bill has contributed to numerous texts, monographs and journals and his particular interests include educational psychology, interpersonal effectiveness, organisational development and Christian leadership within the Catholic tradition.

Tony Burton

Tony Burton is the Director Development in the Faculty of Education at Queensland University of Technology. He is a registered psychologist and teacher and coordinates and teaches counselling in the Faculty. He has worked as a psychologist, teacher and manager, and has consulted widely in the public and private sectors. He has presented numerous workshops about communication skills as they apply to both personal and organisational effectiveness, and is coauthor of *Building Personal Effectiveness*. Tony's special interests include improving interpersonal and organisational communication to enhance positive outcomes.

Introduction

People Skills: guiding you to effective interpersonal behaviour is for those people who are serious about exploring some of the fascinating dynamics of interpersonal effectiveness at a relatively beginning level. It would be erroneous to believe that there are universal truths to be conveyed, and arrogant to advocate that we as fellow "travellers" on this journey of life can provide the answers. Our hope is that we can highlight adequately a little of the field and, where possible, introduce you to your own possibilities for exploration so that your perceptions and pursuits may be more informed, directed and energised.

We begin by establishing a context for interpersonal development and then suggest a basic model for interpersonal functioning. In the chapters that follow, we apply this to reflections about the self, the significance of basic skills for advancing effective relationships, working effectively in groups, thriving in organisations, the challenge of personal leadership and valuing renewal as an ongoing process in interpersonal development.

The format within each chapter is designed to be supportive of our core goals: to share meaning with a sense of application to the real world. The material has been designed to be accessible by a "multi-aged classroom" and includes both theoretical concepts and practical applications. The themes are introduced by key terms and developed by related concepts. The short quotation that begins each chapter offers you an opportunity to reflect creatively.

PEOPLE SKILLS guiding you to effective interpersonal behaviour

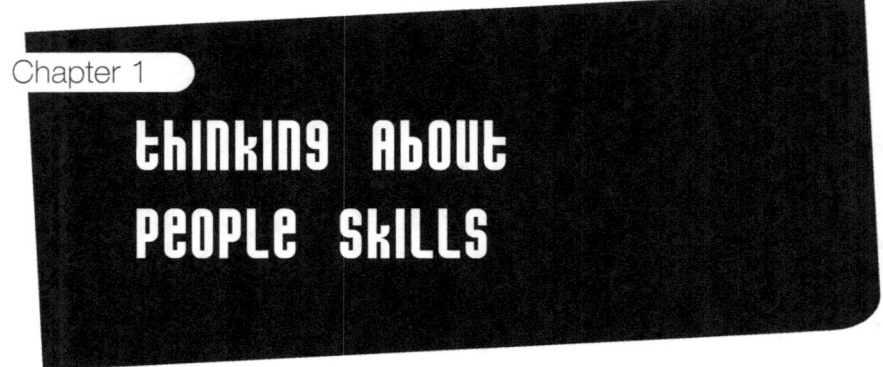

Chapter 1
thinking About People Skills

The unexamined life is not worth living
— Heraclitus

Focusing

Pass it on

> A person we knew and admired was renowned within his community for his ability to get to the heart of the matter, largely through his simple but powerful reflections. His life was characterised by reaching out to others. Herbert Victor Tildesley (1905–1997) epitomised the classical "giver" who always put others first and was unceasing in generosity of all forms. One of his typical responses to those who would express appreciation for his kindness was simply, "just pass it on". The content of this work is offered in the same vein. To the extent that we have been offered something of value, and have been able to reflect and choose what has been helpful, we too endeavour simply to pass it on.

Thinking Metacognitively

Those who engage regularly in an activity, such as sport, can become obsessed to the point of not just "playing a game" but becoming so committed that significant time is spent just thinking about it. For example, sportspeople often become so fixated on the experience that they "stand back" and think about what the task actually involves. As a consequence of this action they may go on to analyse

their style and maybe progress to rehearsing a better way of approaching what might normally be a complex activity.
The process of separating oneself from a task in order to examine it is a process of metacognition — a means for reflection that entails looking objectively at something without actually engaging in the process itself.

Within the discipline of education, teachers can use this technique of thinking metacognitively in order to facilitate learning. For instance, in the area of literacy development, beginning readers can be encouraged to stand back from the print and make some observation about the task of "reading" itself. That is, they can be encouraged to pause and recognise the type size, font changes, repetition of language, left-to-right sequencing and the structure of a paragraph from the top to the bottom of the page. In this way the process of reading becomes more readily understood and the skills involved in the process become more accessible.

The development of people skills is a metacognitive process because the individual is challenged to stand outside a situation and analyse the dynamics of what is observed or spoken about. It is a process of deeper reflection. The act of reflection allows for a person's experience to be brought to a situation, and, with the application of knowledge and skills, to make a meaningful contribution to the life and experience of self and others. It involves thinking about what is unfolding, which thereby provides a basis for interpersonal understanding.

Saying it Simply

Most writers will advance that the first, and often the most difficult, task is that of identifying the core theme around which the material will be gathered. Once having settled on the theme the task then becomes one of explaining it simply. An experienced academic colleague of ours has said to his students that it is a process not unlike retelling "Goldilocks and the Three Bears". In other words, identify the simple story line and allow it to unfold in the presentation. Begin with the "bones" and allow the "flesh" to be added with some reasonable structure.

The theme of this work on people skills is one of the most fundamental aspects of our human functioning: our wholeness and connection. This takes place within our personal being and in our relationships with others.

Not only are our individual natures unique, so too are our relational experiences. We are intimately connected to other people, life's events, institutions and challenges so that a variety of environments inform and change us. Understanding the nature of these engagements and being in a position to use this knowledge in productive ways is crucial to our development; that is, to be able to think about, intervene and improve in the context of others, groups, organisational life, leadership responsibilities and continuous renewal.

We possess a personal ecology (our cognitive, affective, physical and spiritual dimensions) and we function in numerous environments with others. This text explores these ecologies and seeks to unravel some of the complexity and dynamics at work within them.

Facilitating the Continuing Journey

The experience of this text does not begin with the first few pages, or for that matter, the entirety of the material. Our belief is that one never comes to an educative experience empty-handed, and that what the teacher should do is recognise and engage the wisdom that already exists and so add value to the journey already begun. Hence, what this text offers is a stimulus to reflect and build on the experience of your life. The text presumes that you already know a great deal about people skills as people engagement has been part of the "fabric" of your life.

Learning occurs when interpretation happens and your own ideas are enhanced. The extent of this learning is only tested when this interpretation is applied in some practical way; for example, it could be the first time you are able to use the concepts to reduce conflict or are able to understand better a group's function. Whether you can use these ideas to enhance your life's journey will be evidence of the success or otherwise of what we teach you.

Key Terms

Prior to proceeding with a discussion of people skills there are a few basic terms and concepts that demand attention. These are at the core of interpersonal development and serve to remind us of why we should bother with people skills.

Mind
The mind is an arena of thought based on selection and interpretation of experience that is secured through perception.

Feelings
Feelings are electrochemical reactions to thoughts that are transmitted around the body.

Body
The body is the physical self that is able to sense, move and carry out behaviours in response to thoughts, and the feelings that are precipitated by thoughts.

Community
Community is the presence and experience of people interacting as a consequence of their bodies, minds and feelings.

Consciousness
Consciousness is the awareness of self and the environment as a consequence of the selection and interpretation of information.

Unconsciousness
Unconsciousness is a body of stored experience, perceptions, thoughts and feelings that are not recognised at the level of consciousness.

Perception
Perception is the ability to receive information through the senses of touch, taste, smell, vision and hearing, and the "sixth" sense of intuition.

Concept Development

The primary theme of this text is that people skills are significant and that some exploration of them in terms of a changing context, education, prevention, development and connection is helpful to interpersonal relationships and quality of life.

Context
One of the few statements we can make with some certainty these days is that our lives are becoming increasingly complex, busier and more pressured. Moreover, the environments impacting on us are undergoing change. To be able to deal with this feeling of being rushed in a rapidly changing world we need to become sensitive to the complexity around us, as well as develop the necessary skills to meet the challenges with confidence. Rather than being passive and reactive within these complex social systems, our behaviour needs to reflect proactivity and skilled engagement with a changing and challenging world.

Education
The concept of "feed a man a fish and you feed him for a day, but teach him how to fish, and you feed him for a lifetime" is applicable to what we want to achieve with this book. Education, drawn from the Latin, *educare*, means leading people out of places of unknowing to circumstances of growth and development. Within a contemporary context this is pursued through facilitation and

support for the development of skills and behaviours that can be life-long and life-giving. As the slogan recounts: "The sage on the stage is now replaced by the guide on the side."

Prevention

The terms "upstream and downstream" interventions are sometimes used to differentiate two types of behaviours that are focused on people supporting and assisting other people. The terms are usually associated with the metaphor of the river (life's journey) and the difficulties that people experience as they travel.

A man is sitting on the banks of a stream when he sees a person in trouble and, without hesitation, he goes to the rescue. He swims to the person, secures his attention and reliance, returns to shore and pursues the necessary resuscitation and recovery techniques. The rescue is successful, but before too much time elapses another "body" comes floating by. Once again the man on the bank rescues the person in the water. Again and again the task is performed until the "rescuer" becomes too worn out to rescue anymore, and ultimately decides to go "upstream" to explore and intervene before the trouble starts. In a similar mode, this text tries to offer sufficient knowledge and skills so that upstream calamity can be prevented, thereby reducing the need for downstream intervention.

Development

How often do we consider just how lucky we are? This is not a luck based on winning the Lotto or having a good day at the races, but rather the good fortune in just being alive. Some people are never fully happy. It is always a matter of my next million, my third car, a new beach house, the ultimate promotion or a new business venture. In other words, what they have is never enough. However, for others, just being alive, waking up and being given another day is sufficient for them to feel happy. What becomes important in life is the satisfaction that is derived not from material things, but the happiness that arises from being and experiencing the richness of life. All people are journeying in life and at the heart of this journey is authentic human development: the capacity to learn and grow from experience, which has as its ultimate reward contentment, peace and happiness.

Connectedness

Environmental scientists have long told us that unless we recognise our reliance on nature our long-term prospects of survival will diminish. Pollution, ozone reduction and toxic waste are facts that tell us more and more of our global interdependence and of our delicate positioning within the expanding universe. Within the arena of our social existence we have always recognised that we are not alone and that the experience of development is dependent upon others. Primarily, who we are is defined by the nature of our experience of others, who provide us with the information about life, living and ways of behaving that constitute our social and cultural norms.

Our processes for receiving and dealing with information are shown in the ways that we take in information (through perception), select and interpret what the conscious and unconscious self determines, give expression to this information in our rational mind and then experience the nature of this thought through feelings. Our reactions and movement within the community give added expression to this behaviour, which in turn can serve to alter or reinforce the thoughts, feelings and behaviours that were precipitated initially. The next chapter will detail this interconnectedness that exists among your mind, feelings, behaviours and interpersonal relationships, all of which constitute the basis of interpersonal behaviour.

Chapter 2

Functioning in the Real World: A Framework for Interpersonal Development

> People feel disturbed not by things, but by the views they take of them
> — Epictetus

Focusing

Why do we Get Exam Jitters?

Paul was soon to sit a very important exam. As the big day drew closer and closer, he found himself becoming increasingly anxious. He was not sleeping well and was irritable with those around him. When he was asked why he was nervous, Paul replied that it was because the exam was imminent. Thus, he attributed his feelings (anxiety) and lack of sleep (behaviour) to the event (the exam). But why was his friend, Tom, not anxious? Also, why had Paul not been very anxious before his previous exam if exams caused him anxiety?

Tom's attitude was easy to explain. He knew the work and therefore had no need to feel anxious. Paul had not been anxious before the last exam because he knew the work and felt no anxiety about failing. Paul's counsellor asked him how he might feel and behave if he thought the exam was going to be extremely easy. He said he would feel relaxed (feeling) and probably watch a bit more TV (behaviour). How was it, asked his counsellor, that his feelings and behaviour in response to the same exam could be so different? Paul began to understand that his thoughts about the exam dictated his response, not the exam itself. To put it another way, the consequence (feeling and behaviour) about the exam (event) depended on his perception of it (thought). So, did the exam (event) cause the anxiety (feeling) or was it something else?

We can now look more closely at how our emotions and behaviours in a situation are affected by our thoughts about that situation. This relationship is described as the cognitive-behavioural framework. It is a way of examining events, beliefs and consequences that allows for understanding and potential change in our behaviours.

Key Terms

A = Activating Event
This is the event that acts as a stimulus to what follows but does not cause it.

B = Beliefs
This is the belief we have about the activating event and includes how we think about it, our attitude to it and what we say to ourselves about it.

C = Consequences (Emotional and Behavioural)
These are the feelings and behaviours that occur largely as a result of our beliefs.

MODEL

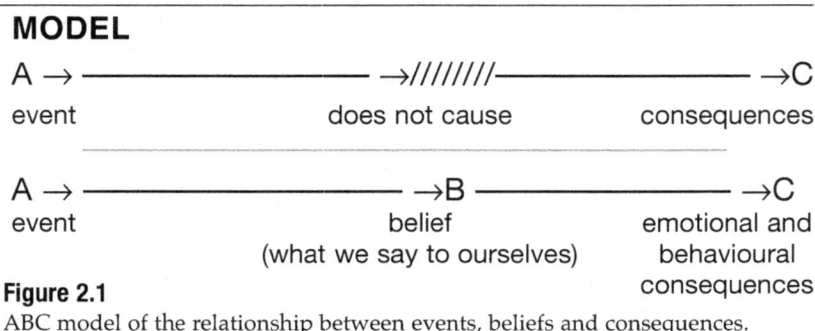

Figure 2.1
ABC model of the relationship between events, beliefs and consequences.

Concept Development

The acceptance that cognition (what we think and then say to ourselves) is the major determinant of emotion and behaviour provides us with the understanding that we can control our emotions and behaviours rather than allow them to control us. This implies that we have choice and can make changes that will help to modify our emotions. A number of key concepts are related to this idea.

What we Say to Ourselves

What we say to ourselves about the event rather than the event itself has the greatest impact on our behaviour and feelings.

Must and Should

Should and must are two of the most destructive words in the English language. They suggest that if you do not act in a certain way then you have failed. But shouldn't we strive for perfection? We can strive to do our best all of the time and some of the time we may even do some things perfectly, but not all of the time.

If your partner leaves you must, or at the very least should, be unhappy. If you say to yourself that you can't stand being without them and that you must be a worthless person for them to leave you then of course you will feel very unhappy and probably depressed. If, on the other hand, you think that it might be more peaceful because the fighting will stop, you may still feel sad and miss them, but you may not feel and act so distressed.

Recognising our Imperfection

We know that humans are imperfect. So how can we expect these imperfect beings to act perfectly all of the time? The answer is we can't, and if we expect them to we will be continually disappointed both in ourselves and others.

We are imperfect products of both our temperament and our upbringing (nature and nurture), but this does not mean that for the rest of our lives we have no power to modify the way that we respond to events. For example, if your father always got very angry when he applied for a job and did not get it, this should not explain your reaction to failure. Another way he could have perceived such an event might have been that it was not meant to be, that it was a learning experience for next time, or that he was not a good match for the job. The reason your father felt angry is probably because he *thought* he was rejected or inadequate, which led to his feelings of anger. If he could have modified his *beliefs* about what happened, he may have been disappointed rather than angry. Similarly, we can modify our thinking to be more flexible, thereby leading to more constructive and beneficial relationships.

No Obligation

We are a product of both nature and the way we are nurtured, but that does not mean that we are obliged to think and behave in a predetermined way for the rest of our lives. We can alter our thinking, and, in turn, create positive behaviours and feelings that are more productive.

REFLECtION 2.1

Bill came from a poor family that valued people who worked hard and got ahead in life. Earning money was the man's responsibility where Bill came from, and emotional care of the family and self was not considered important for the man. Bill got his father's approval by working hard, earning a lot of money and providing well for his family — the bigger the house and the more possessions the better. Bill worked 14 hours per day for seven days a week to ensure that he was successful.

Some years later Bill's father died. Following his father's death, Bill continued to follow the same lifestyle, even though he had realised by then that this was not the lifestyle he wanted. He missed seeing his children grow up and his marriage had experienced difficulties. He had seen friends' marriages fail and he really did not want this to happen to him. When asked why he did not cut back on work and spend more time with his family he said he would feel uncomfortable doing so even though he wanted to. It appears he may be still seeking approval from his father and continuing to be obligated to a mode of work based on the expectation of a significant other.

Conscious and Unconscious Thoughts

Both conscious and unconscious thoughts impact on our feelings and behaviours. You may remember a time when your thinking about something caused you to become anxious about it. You may also remember times when you were anxious without any apparent thoughts prior to the anxiety. These subconscious thoughts are generally ingrained beliefs or attitudes about how we, others and the world should behave. Take, for example, the belief that parents should be totally responsible for the behaviour of their children. This belief may cause a mother or father to become anxious about things they may not be able to control. These subconscious thoughts often cause instant reactions to events.

REFLECtION 2.2

Consider the mother whose young child throws a tantrum in a supermarket. When the child acts badly because he cannot have what he wants, the mother may feel that people might view her as a bad parent if she allowed the incident to continue. She feels responsible for her child's behaviour and concerned about how others might view her. If you asked her, she would say that she did not think she was responsible, but her actions tell us that she was subconsciously influenced by her beliefs.

Dysfunctional Thinking

Some of the characteristics of dysfunctional thinking include the following:
- It distorts reality and often involves irrational ways of viewing the behaviour of yourself, others and the world.
- It creates emotions that are more extreme and that may persist longer than you would generally expect given the activating event.
- It tends to prevent the achievement of goals and interferes with the development of a happy life.

Distorting Reality

The major ways that people misinterpret situations and distort reality incorporate the following (Beck, 1988):
- Mind reading: jumping to conclusions about what others are thinking.
- Fortune telling: treating beliefs about the future as realities.
- Black and white thinking: seeing extremes with no middle ground.
- Overgeneralising: taking one behaviour and thinking it represents the total person.
- Filtering: seeing the negatives and ignoring the positives.
- Personalising: thinking that things are connected to you even when they are not.
- Emotional reasoning: thinking that the way you feel is the way it is.

Irrational Ratings

We also *rate* events. Irrational ratings can involve *catastrophising*, *demanding* and *people rating* (Ellis, 2002).

Catastrophising. This involves "awfulising" and "I can't stand it" comments. Awfulising is rating something as terrible and awful. Saying "I can't stand it" is telling yourself that you cannot tolerate things. Sometimes these two things go together and it is often the unpleasant *feelings* rather than the *event* that we can't stand. The most common problem associated with this combination is *low frustration tolerance*.

Demanding. This is where the preferences that we all have become *demands*. Demands are usually either *musterbations* or *moralising*. Musterbation is turning a desire into an absolute need: "I must get a perfect result in the exam." Moralising is thinking in *shoulds* and *oughts*. These occur as a result of turning guidelines for life into unbreakable rules, for example, "the world should be fair". While a *need* is a survival necessity, such as food or water, a preference is what we desire and a demand is a desire that we say we must have.

People rating. This is where you rate or evaluate the whole of yourself or others based on some behaviour or characteristic that you or they possess. It is called judging the whole by the part. For example, you are a totally bad person because you do one bad thing. Accepting the whole of yourself, including all your characteristics, both positive and negative, is described as self-acceptance. Rather than rate *people* we should rate *behaviours* (Ellis, 1992).

APPLICATION

Functional Thinking and Living
Some ideas supporting functional thinking and living include the following:
1. Learn to observe your own thinking. Practise asking yourself what you said to yourself about an event or person that caused you to feel and act the way you did.
2. List the occasions where you feel or act in an extreme or dysfunctional way and try to examine what type of dysfunctional thinking you are doing. (e.g., catastrophising).

3. Examine the exaggerated language you are using in your thoughts and try to modify it (e.g., never or always could be changed to mostly doesn't or generally does).
4. Ask yourself the question, "Where is the evidence to support this thinking?"
5. Ask yourself the question, "Does this thinking make sense?"
6. Ask yourself the question, "Is this thinking helpful to me?"
7. Make yourself a catastrophe scale and put the current situation into perspective. For example, if 100 on the catastrophe scale for you is nuclear war and human devastation, 50 may be having a major but not physically harmful car accident and 1 might be having a fuzzy TV. Write your own items for 100, 50 and 1, then place the current situation in its place on the line (see Figure 2.2).
8. Tell yourself that emotional distress, no matter how uncomfortable, can be tolerated.
9. Learn to accept realistic criticism of specific behaviours but not total disapproval of you.

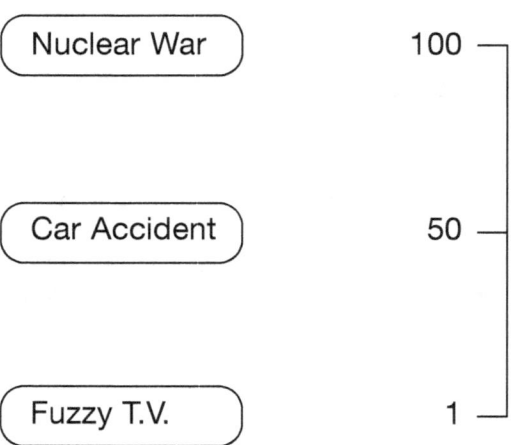

Figure 2.2
Example of a catastrophe scale.

10. Reward yourself with things you *want* not because you *deserve* them.
11. Use rational imagery to practise thinking and acting more functionally.
12. Use the circle approach to look at both positive and negative aspects of yourself and others (see Figure 2.3).

Using the diagram in Figure 2.3, place the positive and negative aspects of yourself or others in the various sectors of the circle. Notice that whomever you choose has both characteristics. Challenge yourself by choosing someone you think has few redeeming qualities and try to find and focus on their positive aspects.

Conclusion

We can choose how we function in the real world. It is not the events or others who cause us to be emotionally upset. Rather, it is the way we think about or interpret the event that dictates our emotional and behavioural response.

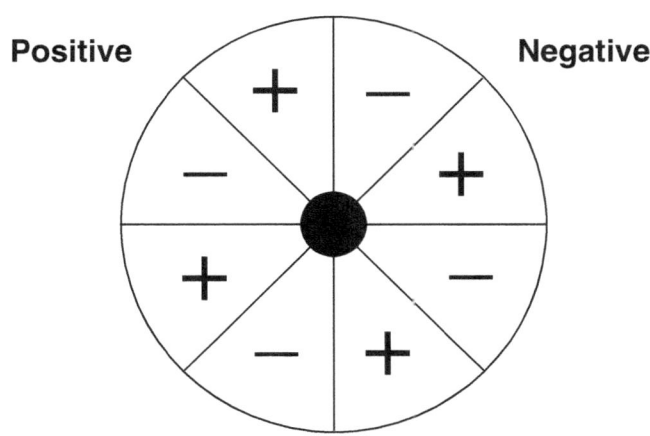

Figure 2.3
The circle approach helps you to look at the positive and negative aspects of yourself and others.

Once you accept this you can understand that it is you who are responsible for your feelings. It is also true that you are capable of modifying your thinking and, as a result, modifying your emotional responses. Thus, it is your choice how you function in the world.

Changing your thinking is at least as difficult as changing your level of physical fitness. To achieve and maintain physical fitness we expect to have to monitor our diet and exercise on a daily basis. Even when we do this, we accept that it will take time to achieve our goals. The same principles apply with our cognitive and emotional fitness program. Continue to work hard and consistently and you will achieve your goal of functioning effectively.

Chapter 3
HOW "I" FUNCTION: the Effective self

Begin with yourself; do not begin out there
— David Hunt

Focusing
Knowing Yourself

> A well-known politician was dating a female actor and was considering marriage. He was concerned that the connections she had made in her occupation may be dubious and come back to haunt him in his career. To ensure that this was not the case he asked a private detective to follow and report on her with the understanding that the detective did not know who he was. The detective reported back that the woman's contacts were generally upstanding citizens, apart from a politician of dubious repute whom she had been dating.

The parable of the politician reveals something about how individuals perceive the world. On the one hand the politician was prosperous, committed and careful. He was sure about his affection for the actress and knew most of her qualities. On the other hand he possessed an implicit acceptance of himself, but appeared to have a blind spot about his own standing in the community. His understanding of self did not reflect the perception of others and neither was he confident nor trusting enough of the woman he wished to marry.

While we may not be sympathetic towards the politician, coming to an understanding of self is not a simple process. It may sound straightforward and appear achievable but, as we will highlight, it is complex, subject to alteration and perhaps never fully achievable. The "journey within" is the most significant in life and also the most challenging. In coming to some understanding of self, it is possible to establish a foundation for our interaction with others, identify our own strengths and generate a confidence that arises from being in touch with our own experience and wisdom. It will also provide a platform for change and permit growth.

Key Terms

The important terms to understand in relation to yourself are the self, self-concept and self-esteem.

The Self
The self is the sum total of all you can call your own: inclusive of body, possessions, relationships, reputation, family and so on.

Self-concept
Your self-concept includes the perception or image of yourself in terms of ability, value, worth, limitations and so on.

Self-esteem
Self-esteem is your satisfaction with or evaluation of your self-concept.

Self-image
Self-image is how you see yourself from a physical perspective.

Concept Development

Self-concept

How does the self-concept develop? It may follow a pattern similar to, and be heavily influenced by, biological growth (nature).

A second approach depicts the self as a social self, which emerges from the maturing self interacting with the environment (nurture). In this model, the environment plays a particular role in shaping the self, irrespective of the body's biological development. Neither of these positions, nature nor nurture, recognises the constant interaction between the developing self and the environment. Biological determinants and environment do interact. The interaction results in the formation of a growth matrix that is continually influenced by biological and environmental factors.

However the self-concept develops, it is probable that all behaviour is related to developing or maintaining a positive self-concept. For example, if your self-concept is that of a hard-working individual, then your behaviour will be focused on reinforcing this image. One implication of this is that if the self-concept is the organised and optimal perception of the self, it can be resistant to change as the person strives to maintain a consistent image. Equally, if the self-concept is negative, for example, "I can never play that game", then the person's behaviour would correspond with that perception. They would either avoid activities that would alter the perception or even take steps that would deliberately result in failure and thereby reinforce the belief. In some instances a belief system can be so powerful that the person will see, hear and interpret only what confirms their self-concept and system of beliefs. Reinforcement of the self-concept is therefore an important factor in our interpersonal lives and can greatly influence how we think, feel and act.

REFLECTION 3.1

In a typical day a young mother engages in a range of activities so broad that her self journeyed in many directions. She was a woman, wife, mother, taxi driver, cook, financier, cleaner, lover, intellectual and friend. How many different types of self do you have? Reflect upon your own typical day and identify how many different expressions of self appeared? Were your images of self different or similar?

Perception and Social Conditioning

The effects of our experience and consequent perception of ourselves, others, actions or events are very powerful determinants of the self-concept. We seldom can be totally objective because we are all the products of unique patterns of growth and development. No two individuals are the same and present perception is influenced by development and what is currently held in each person's "mind's eye".

APPLICATION

To illustrate this point about perception being linked to previous experience we would like you to undertake a simple task.

The first step is simply to choose one exercise, One or Two. In both activities you are asked to imagine yourself as a young, enthusiastic and creative Year 1 class teacher in a middle-class, outer suburban area.

Remember you must choose only ONE exercise. Do not look at the other exercise.

Exercise One: (Literacy skill development)

"Big Ears" has been the class pet for almost seven months. She is a two-year-old white rabbit who was initially brought to school by one of the students for a "describe your pet" activity and afterwards was adopted by the class. Each day, students are rostered to clean her cage, provide food and water and generally look after her wellbeing. The class has become attached to Big Ears and you are hoping that it might help those struggling with their literacy skills to write a story about her.

Reflect for a moment on how you might proceed in using "Big Ears" to stimulate talking, writing, listening and reading for a group of Year 1 students.

Irrespective of whether you did Exercise One or Two, now turn to page 26.

Exercise Two: (Farmyard Excursion)
Science and environmental education are part of your curriculum and you have decided to visit a nearby tourist centre, "Old MacDonalds's", which specialises in introducing children to farmyard animals. You decide to take your class to "Old MacDonald's" but you are alerted to the possible antics students might engage in around the duck pond. The principal has pointed out that the students in previous years have become very excited by the friendly ducks, so much so that when feeding them they have followed them into the shallow pond. Parents have generally objected to students getting wet, so you are asked to take precautions.

Reflect for a moment on what you might do to restrict students from chasing the ducks into the shallows.

Irrespective of whether you did Exercise One or Two, now turn to page 26.

For those who did Exercise One it is likely that you saw a rabbit when you looked at the picture, while those who did Exercise Two probably saw a duck.

The issue is not whether the picture is of a rabbit or a duck, but that you were likely to perceive either, depending on the conditioning that had occurred through the exercise. This demonstrates how your previous experiences and associations can influence how you perceive an event. Our experiences condition the meanings that we attribute to events, people, places and things.

The dynamics of what occurs in social interactions is similarly influenced by our experience. We can infer motives and intentions to actions that may, at best, be speculative and impressionistic. For example, if we see two people waving hands, using aggressive language and raised voices. We may think that they are in conflict; however, it may be that one person is describing how someone else behaved to the other person, or perhaps it is the normal way for people to interact in a particular culture.

Understanding the self, and the development of the self-concept, does come largely from social contact. Our susceptibility to influences will vary with our stage in life (infancy/childhood/adolescence/adulthood) and will be dependent on the significant others that influence us: parents, siblings, peers, partners and teachers. Developing an understanding of your self-concept and how it grows is important, because unless you can understand your self-concept, you cannot fully reflect on what is happening in your life and relate to outside events with heightened awareness and skill.

REFLECtION 3.2

Two priests were walking along a footpath drinking out of a bottle of beer. The people who saw them were horrified and one complained to them about their unacceptable behaviour. They laughed and said that they were not really priests, but were on their way to a fancy dress party. What would you have thought if you were there? Would your perception of the people being priests have changed your view of events? Can you remember a similar situation where your perceptions were not reality?

Self-awareness

How often do we hear that in the pursuit of our goals we must start with the self? This means that you should first reflect upon and analyse what it is that gives you life, energy and motivation. This is the starting point for real learning and achievement.
The process is about taking time to stop and reflect, enter your inner life in order to connect with what you feel and believe, and thereby set a direction for continuing your life's journey with knowledge and intention. It involves identifying and living with spirit in a way that connects beliefs, values, intentions and action.

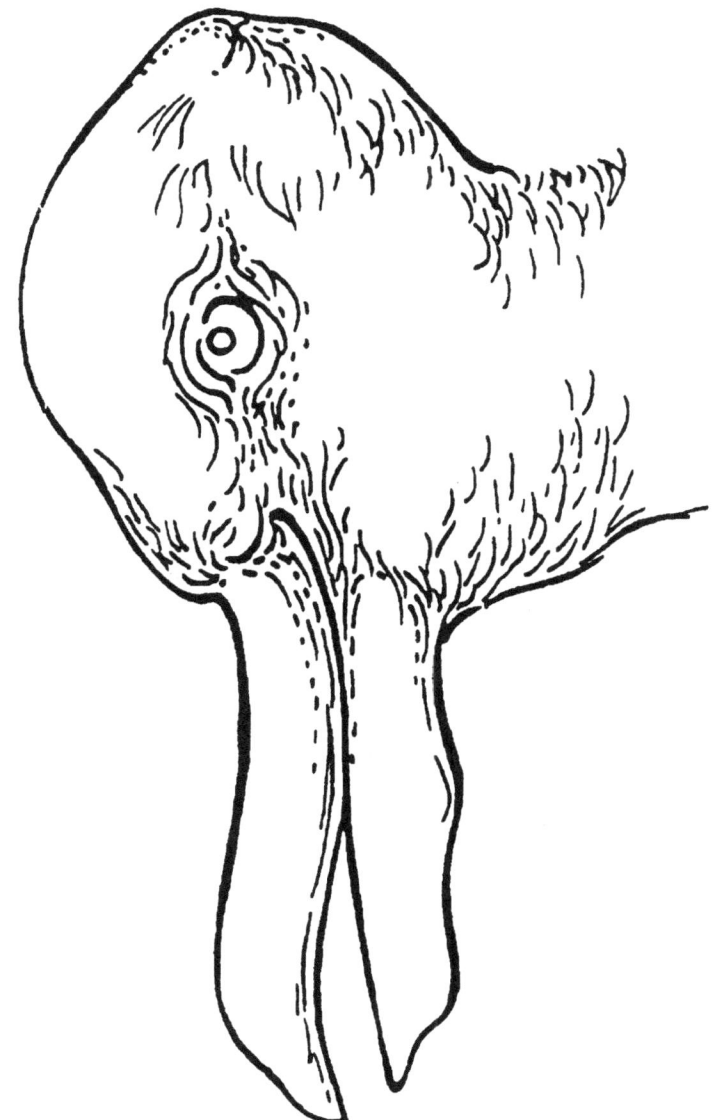

Figure 3.1
Study the picture carefully, turn the book around if you wish, use your imagination and generally take time with the image.

A commitment to personal journeying, reflecting on the self in the ordinary and the everyday, does not come easily. Life can so easily become a merry-go-round of events and routine that evades reflection and blanks out what is most important. How much time do we spend in touch with the core of ourselves, making sense of our lives, and deciding on our ideal directions? While we observe the physical side of ourselves repeatedly, we seldom take time to look more closely and actually observe the richness of our inner selves.

Facilitating Self-awareness

A figurative model for facilitating self-awareness is the device developed by Joseph Luft and Harry Ingham (Luft, 1969) called the JOHARI window. The model shows how knowledge of the self can be developed through self-disclosure and feedback from others.

The first step in the development of the model is to imagine that everything about yourself (likes, presentation, relationships, goals, secrets, needs, motivation, etc.) can be represented as known or unknown to you. Similarly, we can also divide the self that is known to others into two parts: known and unknown. Through a combination of information from the self and others the JOHARI window can be generated (see Figure 3.2)

The first part, described as the "open" area, represents that part of yourself that is known to both you and others. Part 2 is called the "blind" area, as it depicts what others see but what you do not. The "hidden" area (Part 3) includes those parts that you know but that others are not aware of, and the "unknown" area (Part 4) refers to those aspects of yourself that are not apparent to you or others.

The JOHARI window is a useful tool because it graphically illustrates how complex the self can be and how important it is to possess and use your personal awareness of yourself and your knowledge of yourself from interpersonal relationships. The ideal, relative to the development of self-awareness, is to strive to increase

Formation of the JOHARI Window
SELF-KNOWLEDGE

Things known to self	Things not known to self

OTHERS' KNOWLEDGE OF SELF

Things known to others	Things not known others

		SELF	
		Known	Not Known
OTHERS	Known	Open 1	Blind 2
	Not Known	Hidden 3	Unknown 4

Figure 3.2
The JOHARI window shows how knowledge of the self can be developed through self-disclosure and feedback from others.

our "openness". In achieving this we expand our knowledge of ourselves and allow others to become more aware of the different parts of ourselves as well.

It is through interactions with others, building relationships and being open in them, that we can learn much more about the self. Relationships in the beginning phase are often characterised by considerable "unknown" information, whereas in their developed form they are characterised by the degree of shared meaning or openness that has been achieved. Through interacting in this way our "blind" dimension to self decreases and the "unknown" domain also decreases. What grows is our capacity to be real, aware and honest in our assessment and practice of building good self-awareness.

The importance of gaining self-knowledge by being open was summarised by David Johnson (1986). He depicted openness as arising from recognition, acceptance and trust of self and others. His model of an open relationship is shown in Table 3.1. It comprises being open *with* you and being open *to* you. It demands disclosure of self and it requires acceptance and recognition of others.

REFLECtION 3.3

A man has red hair, blue eyes and is wearing a brown suit. He has bad breath and is secretly addicted to watching silent movies. He is not aware that he has the heart rate of a champion athlete. Consider what his JOHARI window might look like. How would you fill out your own JOHARI window?

Table 3.1
Model of an Open Relationship

Being aware of myself, of who I am, and of what I am like	Being aware of you, who you are, and of what you are like
+	+
Being accepting of myself, aware of my strengths and abilities	Being accepting of you, aware of your strengths and abilities
+	+
Trusting you to accept and support me, to cooperate with me, and to be open with me results in	Being trustworthy by accepting and supporting you, cooperating with you and being open with you results in
+	+
Being open with you, sharing my ideas and feelings, and letting you know who I am as a person	Being open to you, being interested in your ideas and feelings and in who you are as a person
Being open with you + Being open to you = an open relationship	

The "Ideal" Self

Growth in self-understanding takes on additional meaning if we aim towards an ideal. This leads us to ask what is optimal functioning? How do we recognise emotional health? The answers to these questions are very difficult, because what is optimal for one person might not necessarily be optimal for another; people possess different levels of motivation, needs, opportunities and skills. With this in mind we may still want to enquire into whether there are some general characteristics of optimally functioning people.

Perspectives on the ideal self vary with research, philosophy and experience. In a creative and fascinating paper, Ryan, Hawkins and Russell (1992) established a mythical dialogue among three prominent influences in humanistic psychology (Carl Rogers, Viktor Frankl and Abraham Maslow). These three authors are brought together and the larger questions (about life, education and motivation, etc.) are addressed. Their responses to the goals of education give us an idea about the ideal self or growth towards optimal functioning:

> The far goal ... is to grow to the fullest humanness, to the greatest fulfilment and actualisation of their highest potential to their greatest possible stature. In a word, it should help them become actually what they deeply are potentially (Maslow).

> Education must see its principal assignment in refining the individual's conscience — one's only capacity still to find meanings despite the wane of traditions and values (Frankl).

> ... to give learners such control over the methods of being in society that they will become the learning person (Rogers).

For Maslow, growth through actualisation of potential is critical, while Frankl calls for formation of the conscience, and Rogers speaks of developing processes for ongoing learning. Hence, maximising potential, conscience formation and process skills emerge as important. There are others, of course, and given our differing approaches to our learning we would all offer particular positions. However, when reflecting upon a number of views from social sciences writers, certain characteristics of optimally functioning people come to prominence. These people tend to (1) think well of themselves; (2) think well of others; (3) recognise interdependence with others; (4) see themselves in a process of becoming; (5) understand the value of mistakes; (6) develop and hold values related to the welfare of people; (7) live in keeping with their values; (8) accept themselves; (9) live a balanced lifestyle; and, (10) integrate their personal needs (cognitive, social, physical, emotional, spiritual).

Summarising the above is not easy, but in part can be achieved in the terms of "I'm OK. You're OK". Such a position, argued to be the most optimal state psychologically, involves seeing the self and others as equally worthwhile. Self and others are accepted and relationships are happy and meaningful. Life becomes a pilgrimage to the appreciation of self and others.

REFLECtION 3.4

Occasionally we meet someone who approaches being an ideal person. I met a person at a wedding I attended recently who appeared peaceful, well-integrated and composed. He also seemed very aware of the needs of everyone around him and seemed to have an empathy with them. Try to focus on someone you have encountered whom you believed had an ideal self. Why did you feel that way? Try to describe their characteristics.

Clarifying your Self-concept

There are various methods for identifying your self-concept, which can be broadly categorised as formal and informal techniques. The formal processes can be further divided into projective techniques: figure drawing, sentence completion, picture interpretations and self-concept inventories. The projective procedures call for responses to ambiguous tasks, while self-concept report inventories include written or simple checklist responses to a series of questions. Alternatively, informal techniques (conversation, autobiographical journaling and observation) can be used. Each of the methods used to clarify self-concept do possess a specific function and need to be applied with understanding. Perhaps the overriding guideline would be not to use any technique in isolation, and generally to validate outcomes with alternatives.

A simple procedure, combining the formal and informal approaches for determining a view of self comes from a general application of the JOHARI window concept (see Figure 3.3). The task is simple. All it requires is personal reflection and a degree of trust in another person or persons to help establish some of the domains contained in yourself. You must also be committed to documenting these reflections and using them in a balanced fashion. The listing of outcomes is normally done privately and does not necessarily have to be shared. Development would be built up confirming strengths and addressing weaknesses as you journey to desirable goals.

The behaviours that contribute to your self-concept may be changed as you recognise your capacity to plan and determine your life. What is crucial to this is the recognition of the context in which you operate while still being able to determine a "future state" to which you can strive. Central to this achievement is belief in yourself, valuing personal achievements (strengths) and being prepared to address areas for growth in an intentional and decisive fashion.

Building Your Self-esteem

Self-esteem is the value we place on the self-concept. Self-esteem should be encouraged because it generates a positive state of mind, gives encouragement for addressing future issues and provides confidence in your abilities. Two options (and you may wish to

STRENGTH AREAS Perception	**GROWTH AREAS** Perception
SELF	SELF
_____	_____
_____	_____
_____	_____
OTHERS	OTHERS
_____	_____
_____	_____
_____	_____

Figure 3.3
Recording self-concept ideas.

use others) for representing the "positives" about self, and thereby enhancing self-esteem, are simply to record strengths on a "self-esteem tree" or cluster responses by recording particular information on quadrants outlined on a "personal shield". Remember that building self-esteem will depend on personal energy, and what is valued will be defined by personal beliefs, experience and culture. Self-esteem essentially involves how we feel about ourselves, alters with our moods and experiences, and should grow incrementally as we develop. In other words, take time to reflect upon your strengths, do it at a time you feel optimistic and be prepared to alter your comments as you change. The process is dynamic and is designed to give positive outcomes.

Imageing Self

Components of the self can be reinforced through images. Reference to images provides a powerful illustration of a belief or behaviour and facilitates communication about what is most important. In general terms, images can also represent and broaden perspectives and thereby provide insight and material for additional reflection. Above all, images provide a rich and consistent way of recalling a central meaning about an issue or event.

Your image of self and its representation may take any number of forms. Perhaps the most common association would be to link your self-concept with a visual scene of some kind (seascape, landscape, place of quiet, etc.). Alternatively, your self-concept could be linked with a significant other person in your life or perhaps a piece of literature, music, or theatre that continues to have a profound effect on your development. Whatever this image is, it will be useful to identify and use as a means of confirming what you believe you want to achieve or represent in terms of self-concept.

Having selected an image that "speaks to you" it is also valuable to represent it in some symbolic way. Not only is the image then able to be easily brought to mind, but also it has a concrete representation for you and others. Family homes, businesses and recreational facilities often display symbols of meaning and experience as reminders of past achievements, basic values or significant operational practices.

REFLECtION 3.5

One of the most striking examples of an image and symbolic representation of an aspect of self that we have encountered is that of the duck. The individual who alerted us to the power of this image suggested that it represented his approach to business. The image of the duck gliding across a placid, picturesque pond captured something about his approach to the workplace. On reflection we thought that he had selected wisely because his relationships with his clients were smooth, reflective, consistent and unflappable. Little did others know that behind the scenes or "under the water" his activities were fast, diligent, and not always without anxiety or effort. For us, this businessman became known as the duck because so often his approach resembled this image. He now uses the duck as part of his business image, using it to decorate his office and business cards. Following this example, think of the symbols that are most representative of your self-concept. Are these captured in a way to give ready prompting to the regular and routine professional and or personal domains of your interpersonal life?

Conclusion

Knowledge of self is important if we are to grow as individuals in relationships. Put simply, we need to identify first who we are if we are to "walk our talk" where our actions are commensurate with our inner selves (our thoughts, feelings, attitudes and values). The task is one that involves learning about self and utilising this as a basis for action and reflection. Ultimately, it is about you and your self in relationships.

Chapter 4
HOW "WE" FUNCTION: RELATIONSHIP DEVELOPMENT SKILLS

> I keep six honest serving men
> (they taught me all I know),
> their names are what and why
> and when and how and where and who
> — Rudyard Kipling

Focusing

When "I" Becomes "we"

> A young man had just met a beautiful girl whom he wished to marry. Up until now he had lived a bachelor's life of football, drinking, living untidily and generally doing what he wanted when he wanted. He had changed his lifestyle drastically since meeting this girl but was unsure if he could sustain such a change. He had the skills to be part of a "we", but perhaps not the belief in its worth for him.

An understanding of self is fundamental to interpersonal relationships. However, self-knowledge, while important, is not enough. Because we function in a community, we need also to be skilled in our interpersonal life to be able to make the necessary adjustments to the larger social systems affecting us and to operate in ways which are in keeping with our values and beliefs. Our success in living fully, with energy, satisfaction, peace and actualisation, is related to the quality of our relationships and the basic skills that develop and preserve them.

Key Terms

Relationships
Relationships are associations between individuals, which can be manifested as physical (touch, proximity), intellectual (attitudes, values) or psychological (fear, feelings).

Communication
Communication is the transmission of signals that are shared in common by at least two individuals.

Conflict Resolution
Conflict resolution is the recognition and attention to differing perceptions about situations, expectations and negative relational messages that create interpersonal contesting between individuals.

Problem-solving
Problem-solving is the process involved in discovering and applying the most appropriate sequence of alternatives leading to a goal or to an ideal solution.

Concept Development

Relationships

A simple description of interpersonal relationships is that they are a series of interactions between at least two people, expressed at varying levels of intensity, usually over variable periods of time. Interpersonal relationships may reflect a basic awareness of another's presence or existence, or even the exchange of simple ideas and feelings. Mutuality in relationships, however, involves the sharing of one's more personal self and being open to growth induced by the reactions of another person. Determinants of interpersonal relationships can be complex, although what becomes important to interpersonal relationships is the strengthening, or otherwise, of these associations through skills such as communication, problem-solving and conflict resolution.

The power of relationships, and what emerges from them in terms of personal growth, is another of those deeper questions that are usually pondered in psychology tutorials or in some form of group therapy. What most of us know is that relationships are important and influential.

REFLECTION _____ 4.1

There was a famous sports coach who was not a good public communicator. His team members all loved him, but the general public had trouble understanding some of the unpopular decisions he made. I thought he had made many poor decisions and was overrated both as a communicator and a person. I could not understand why the team thought so highly of him. Some time later I organised for him to be a guest speaker at a function. After listening to him talk, and meeting him personally, it became clear to me why people regarded him so highly. He was one of the finest people I had ever met.

Look at a relationship you have formed with someone that progressed to a deeper level. Why did this happen and what possible factors might have led to a different outcome? Also consider whether aspects of personality influenced the relationship.

Relationship Skills

Communication: "Connecting on Common Ground"

The word communication is derived from the Latin *communicare* — "to have in common". Good communication between people supports the transfer of meaning and thereby enhances interpersonal effectiveness. Important factors to remember about communication are that personal intentions do not guarantee accurate reception, and that checking the meaning of messages is critical for accurate exchange. Communication can occur through both verbal and non-verbal channels and is influenced by physical and psychological filters that operate on message output and input.

Message senders and message receivers have different goals, which makes effective communication challenging. The goals of message senders are (a) stating a case clearly and factually, (b) clarifying meaning and making qualifying statements, and (c) seeking responses and being receptive. Message receiver goals include (a) discerning meaning, (b) observing and interpreting signals, and (c) applying appropriate questioning to clarify meaning. Filters, such as attitudes, values, perceptions, experience and self-esteem, which can influence both transmission and reception, also influence communication. Noise caused by physical impediments (ventilation, light, temperature, furniture) and psychological factors (tension, anxiety, insecurity, etc.) can also have a profound effect on the
conveyance of meaning.

Barriers to communication can exist for both the listener and speaker. For the listener, they may include defending one's position, seeking premature entrance into the conversation, being preoccupied with personal concerns, having a closed perspective, and giving advice. Each of these actions/attitudes may distort or deflect stimuli from the speaker. Barriers in the speaking process include an unbalanced relationship, mode of delivery, sending incomplete/incongruent messages, disowning responsibility and inappropriate assumptions about the listener's previous understandings.

Non-verbal data plays a significant role in communication, particularly when there is a difference between content and relationship information contained in verbal messages. Non-verbal communication, often used unconsciously, can strengthen verbal communication by adding to it specific meanings about relationships. For example, feelings can be conveyed non-verbally with a simple gesture, such as smiling. This is usually associated with revealing warmth and openness and underlines powerfully the spoken word. Other relational messages can be communicated in the form of feelings towards the other, feelings about the content of the message and feelings about one's own state of being.

Communication is the most fundamental of the skills associated with interpersonal effectiveness and relationship formation. However, it also needs to be used in conjunction with other interpersonal skills. For instance, one of the most important aspects of communication involves attending to difficulties or breakdowns in relationships. These can involve varying levels of intensity, from mere disagreement, debate, controversy, overt competition or even physical violence.

REFLECTION 4.2

A doctor was talking to a patient about a range of alternatives for managing the problem that he had. She suggested surgery might be the best option and that it had a high percentage success rate. She also suggested a range of other medications and therapies that had a low probability of success. Finally she said that one per cent of people recovered without treatment but, mindful of the patient's age and level of general health, the probability of this occurring was even lower. The patient went home and told his family that no treatment was needed as spontaneous recovery was possible.

Explain this communication in terms of the above model. What other approach could have been used to make the communication more effective and what filters made it more difficult.

Resolving Conflict Through Dispute System Design: "Two Ends to the Middle"

Conflict occurs when there is a perceived divergence of interests and a belief that these competing interests cannot be resolved satisfactorily. Responses to this difference can be manifested in contesting issues, yielding, reluctant acceptance, problem-solving, gossiping, negotiating, violence or avoidance. The alternative is to enter into processes of conflict resolution that seek a constructive solution to the problem in ways that attempt to minimise stress, seek meaningful solutions and, ideally, rebuild relationships. In this way, conflict is often positive and not "all bad", because it can be a creative force for generating energy and personal growth. Conflict that is not confronted can be harmful and debilitating.

There are at least two critical aspects to conflict resolution. The first involves the determination of whether a conflict exists and the establishment of ground rules to address the problem. The second is concerned with the selection and the implementation of strategies to secure resolution by the parties involved.

Assessment of potential conflict entails focusing on issues, such as: Are the parties aware that a conflict exists? Do incompatible/compatible goals point to the degree of conflict? What rewards exist to motivate parties towards a successful resolution? And, what degree of dependence exists between the parties concerned? Depending on the outcomes of these enquiries, the success of a proposed intervention can be established along with the ground rules to guide the resolution. Ground rules might include establishing commitments about the preparedness of parties not to imply blame, jumping to solutions, being prepared to build on ideas and being reflective.
An assessment of these factors and the preparedness of both parties to engage meaningfully in attempts to resolve the conflict are fundamental to achieving constructive outcomes.

A primary strategy for the resolution of conflict is the design of a system for intervention to maximise outcomes acceptable to the parties in conflict. There are three steps to the design process. The first step involves analysing the present system through appropriate "what if" questions; for example, what kinds of disputes are likely to arise? How often? Between whom? What particular procedures for resolution may be worthwhile? The second step entails designing a system with a number of key principles; for example, talking before disputing escalates; focusing on interests; arranging procedures from a low to high-cost sequence; building in loops for negotiation; providing low-cost rights (e.g., arbitration) and power procedures (e.g., voting) as backups; and ensuring that significant others are aware and supportive of the procedures generated. The third step involves implementation and attentiveness to sound procedural processes; for example, providing access to all relevant information; ensuring easy access to the system; making time available for each step; providing flexibility; arranging for ongoing evaluation; and modifying the system as required.

Central to system implementation is its negotiated acceptance by parties involved in the conflict. Moreover, the strength of its success will be affected by the degree of commitment by these same parties. However, because of the emotional engagement associated with the conflict, seeking the assistance of an independent, third party is often necessary. Such a person would need to be acceptable to both parties, possess human relationship skills and be neutral in respect to the identification of outcomes. It is also useful if the third party has no perceived power or status over either participant. This third-party involvement can be either as a mediator (a person who facilitates agreed commitments) or an arbitrator (a person who makes a decision depending on the facts). Arbitrators are often used after mediation has been unsuccessful.

The engagement of a third party can be helpful as "games" or "agendas" can be reduced, as can any imbalance of power between the conflicting parties. The readiness and skill levels of those involved can also be taken into account and an independent assessment of the reality provided. The reliability and validity of information can also be assessed and optimum levels of interaction and tension maintained. Progress in the process can be monitored and "expert" skills put to the service of both parties. Mediation has been successfully applied to a range of situations, including family, commercial, employment, organisational and community disputes.

The application of systematic procedures to secure outcomes acceptable to all parties is similar to the processes used in conflict resolution and problem-solving. The stages are sequential, and to some extent, simple and reasonable. They do, however, require ground rules and an appropriate level of analysis. They also demand communication, negotiation and brainstorming skills, and particularly in the case of conflict resolution, can benefit from the participation of an objective third-party facilitator.

REFLECtION   4.3

The general manager (GM) of a large business was becoming increasingly concerned about the ongoing conflict between two senior managers. They were both capable and previously reasonable people and the now ongoing lack of harmony was affecting the business.

After interviewing the people concerned it became obvious that the real issue was not how to handle the business, which was what they appeared to disagree about, but rather the anxiety about the GM's opinion on how they were performing and its effect on their next promotion. Having identified the real source of conflict a system was put in place for regular feedback on performance and clear and fair promotion guidelines.

Try to identify a recent conflict in which you have been involved. What were the real issues? Did anyone try to solve the conflict before the real issues were recognised? How might you have approached this conflict differently?

Problem-solving: Assessing and Managing Forces

A problem can be defined as a significant deviation from the norm, which is based on what is current and knowing what standards should exist. In other words, a potential problem does not become a problem until its characteristics are compared to current norms or standards and some significant difference is found. Problem-solving involves identifying the gap between the norm and the deviation from it, and taking action because the deviation is unacceptable. As for conflict resolution, there are a number of logical and sequential steps that can be applied to problem-solving.

Recognition of a problem. If a problem is defined as a deviation from what is expected, then it is important that those engaged in the problem-solving activity recognise what is acceptable, know of indicators to assess likely differences, are able to identify gaps, and believe the deviation is of such significance to warrant correction. Even after a problem is recognised, there may still be no need to pursue its resolution. Issues of whether the problem may self-correct, or a belief that change to a situation could be detrimental to the individuals involved, can reduce the motivation to address the problem. Notwithstanding these possibilities, if a problem is recognised, and is viewed as warranting some intervention, then it first needs to be understood and defined.

Problem definition. The challenge and need for problem definition is undertaken, ideally, in three ways: separating issues or themes that constitute the problem, stating clearly what is current and what is being sought, and identifying indicators that will point to problem elimination.

Problem analysis. Problem analysis involves the collection and examination of information (facts and opinions) relative to the problem. Fact and opinion should be separated and if opinion is ventured, facts should be sought to support it. Information, depending on the nature of the problem, may need clustering or ordering in some way. This will help clarify the boundaries to the problem and provide some "opening up" to the complexity that may otherwise be clouded or ambiguous. With complex problems, the breaking up of issues into subcomponents is important.

Problem relationships. Having identified important information about a problem, it is useful to "tease out" relationships to examine whether there are cause and effect mechanisms operating. Such an analysis will help overcome the simplistic approach of eliminating superficial manifestations without going to the possible source for what is causing them. It is important to recognise that removing one cause of a problem may not necessarily produce a desired result, as there may be multiple causes. Hence, if relationships between problems and possible causes can be identified, it is critical to examine them all, as displacement by one contributing factor can lead to the entry of another.

Strategy selection and implementation. In this stage it is critical not to compromise positive outcomes by strategies that, while being potentially optimal, may be too difficult to implement and thereby increase the potential for failure. Hence, strategies that can be achieved and that offer confidence and growth should be considered first. Such criteria as identifying goals, and determining behavioural objectives, time frame, responsibility, people involved, indicators for achievement and review activities will assist in the determination of what is optimal.

Review, reflection and re-focusing. This is almost self-evident, but so often we believe that a problem is solved once a strategy is in place. To ensure that implementation is going to plan, it is necessary to identify formal stages of review by using the indicators nominated, reflecting on the outcomes identified and making adjustments as appropriate. These integrated steps will also need to be documented and recalled periodically in subsequent and related problem-solving processes.

REFLECTION _____ 4.4

The academic staff of a university were faced with the problem of ever-changing roles and an increasing emphasis on undertaking work for which they had never been trained. The problem identified was that the staff required training and support to make the transition. They also needed to be encouraged to participate in the new role, and mentoring was identified as a potential tool for this. Through collaborative consultation with staff it was also suggested that some of the work may be more ably done by others outside the university and that new employees should be competent in the new and important areas.

Try to recall a problem you have solved recently. Analyse it in terms of the steps of the problem-solving process.

The interpersonal skills of communication, conflict resolution and problem-solving, while discussed separately, do have a relationship to one another. Each shares the common purpose of supporting interpersonal effectiveness, specifically within the context of growing and knowing beyond the self.

APPLICATION _____

You have been asked by the principal of a primary community school to assist the school in reviewing its operations. The principal indicates there is a "bit of tension" with the school board. You agree to an exploratory meeting with the principal, during which the following is revealed.

The principal was appointed by the board. The school has operated for five years, during which time there have been three other principals. The appointment of the present principal coincided with the allocation of State Government funding, which required that certain courses be established.

The funding, which provides for the community school to conduct a post-school activities centre, came largely as a result of the initiative of one staff member. This person had been on staff since the school began, was an unsuccessful applicant for the position of principal and is now the staff representative on the school board.

A local businessman donated the capital funds to build the school. He established a trust to provide limited ongoing income. Since his death three years ago, the local community has negotiated with the State Government for recurrent funding and established the school as a legal entity with a school board to oversee its management.

The school has an enrolment of 295 students with a staff (most of whom live locally) of 14 teachers (including the principal) and four ancillary staff.

The school has expanded a little. The preschool was the first expansion and this came after two years of operation. This has extended, as already noted, to a post-school activity centre.

The community school is sited in what could be described as a boom area, with large mortgages and young families.

The school board is constituted by two representatives from each of the three local service groups, the local council member, a school staff representative and two members elected from the local community by the parent body. The office of chairperson is filled by the board members from within their ranks.

As a normal requirement, a government audit of the operation is due to take place in 12 months' time. Future government

Table 4.1

Summary of Intervention Process Design

Intervention Process Design
Description of Situation

Interpretation of Needs
      Communication
      Conflict
      Problems
      Other

Evaluation of Needs
Negotiation of Process (with Client/s)
Process Implementation
Outcomes Evaluation
Future Planning

funding is dependent on the community school realising its goals and objectives.

The overall goal, as stated by the principal, is for a successful outcome from the government operational audit. To achieve this, the community school needs to become more organised, reduce conflict and tension, and build a team in which everyone's needs are met.

Drawing on your appreciation of relationships and the skills of communication, conflict resolution and problem solving, what particular aspects of this situation can you identify?

In your analysis, consider the following:
- What is the nature of the relationships between the people in this situation?
- How much shared meaning is there in communication?
- Are there signs of interpersonal conflict?
- What specific problems exist?
- What would you recommend?
- Where would you start?
- What would you focus on?
- What processes would you suggest?

The key to resolving the problems raised in this case study rests with the appropriate design of processes to meet the presenting issues. Use Table 4.1 as a guide to design your intervention.

Conclusion

Communication, conflict resolution and problem-solving skills represent important "tools" in the development of interpersonal relationships. Central to their application is the overall context in which they are used and the design of the intervention in which these tools' potential can be explored.

Chapter 5
HOW "GROUPS" FUNCTION: GROUP PROCESS DEVELOPMENT

> No man is an island entire of itself;
> every man is a piece of the continent,
> a part of the main
> — John Donne

Focusing
Play for Each Other

A basketball coach was very impressed with the skill level of his team. Everyone was very competent at passing, shooting, defending and all the other skills that appeared important to winning a game. Before the match the coach told the team that if they each played to the best of their ability, they had a good chance of winning. More importantly, though, he said that it was the combination of the entire team that would have the greatest impact on the outcome. Play for each other and operate as a group and your individual skills will be multiplied many times and your performance will surely improve.

The story of the basketball team and their need to work cooperatively to secure a common goal is characteristic of the behaviour sought within groups: individuals share their wisdom and experience in order to achieve an outcome beneficial to all. The task, however, while simply defined, is difficult to realise because working together in groups is complex, demanding, potentially frustrating and always dynamic.

Key Terms

Group Stages
Group stages are natural stages a group will move through because of the individual, interpersonal and whole group dynamics that operate when group processes and tasks are commenced.

Group Interpersonal Dynamics
Group interpersonal dynamics are the nature of interactions between members of a group as they operate individually and collectively.

Entitativity
Entitativity is the extent to which a group is a group. Groupness, or entitativity, is based on the structure, interaction and interdependence that exists within the group.

Syntality
Syntality is the personality of the group that is related to the level of feeling, emotion, cohesion, friendliness and cooperation present among members.

Synergy
Synergy is the level of energy available to the group for its group activities. Synergy is used for the purpose of group maintenance (relationship building) and group tasks.

Group Intervention
Group intervention is a process of identifying dysfunctional group behaviour and taking appropriate steps to move towards the ideal.

Concept Development

Stages of Group Development

Group development is an accepted phenomenon in organisational and interpersonal development literature. While different names can be attached to the stages of group development, there is agreement among researchers that there are about five stages. Stages may be characterised in terms of the major processes or tasks being confronted by the group and the characteristics or interpersonal relationships that arise (see Table 5.1).

Stages One to Five reveal how groups typically approach tasks and operate interpersonally. The general comparisons listed in Table 5.2 reinforce the discreteness of each stage as much as capturing the elements within each.

Table 5.1
Elements of Group Development

Stage	Major Processes	Characteristics
One	Development of relationship bonds, exchange of information, and orientation toward others and the situation.	Tentative interactions, polite discourse, concern over ambiguity and silences.
Two	Dissatisfaction with others, competition among members, disagreement over procedures, conflict.	Criticism of ideas, interruption of speakers, poor attendance and hostility.
Three	Development of group structure, increased cohesiveness and harmony, and establishment of roles and relationships.	Agreement on rules, consensus-seeking, increased supportiveness, and "we" feeling.
Four	Focus on achievement, high task orientation and emphasis on performance and productivity.	Decision-making, problem-solving, increased cooperation and decreased emotionality.
Five	Termination of duties, reduction of dependency and task completion.	Regret, increased emotionality and disintegration.

Table 5.2
Three Forms of Expressing Group Development

Stage	Relationships	Tasks
Forming	Security	Orientation
⇓	⇓	⇓
Storming	Acceptance	Dissatisfaction
⇓	⇓	⇓
Norming	Responsibility	Resolution
⇓	⇓	⇓
Performing	Work	Production
⇓	⇓	⇓
Mourning	Closing	Termination

As groups develop in accordance with the natural unfolding of task and relationship factors, particular developmental tasks that need to be addressed within each stage can be identified. As these are achieved, subsequent stages can occur with a solid foundation having been established. If these tasks are not dealt with effectively they can present obstacles detrimental to group formation. Group formation is also dependent on individuals being prepared to work for the group, not just themselves, and in doing so, being open to the needs of others. Working effectively in groups can demand much at interpersonal and personal levels.

Drawing from the particular developmental tasks, and identifying some of the interpersonal challenges associated with them, it becomes possible to match group processes that can support group development. Table 5.3 shows a simple breakdown of these interrelated factors and a preliminary linkage between each.
What is important is that as we come to appreciate more the varying stages a group will inevitably pass through, the more likely we are to understand the interpersonal dynamics that are occurring. Armed with this knowledge we can assess the interpersonal challenges being experienced by group members and thereby attend to them through either structured experiences or simply by being sensitive to them.

Table 5.3
Aligning the Dynamics Operative in Groups

Stage	Tasks	Interpersonal Challenges	Formation Experiences
Forming	Get acquainted Set boundaries Build trust	Risk by being open Commit to task Put aside self-interest	Getting acquainted Setting ground rules
Storming	Personal sharing Group cohesiveness	Listen attentively Risk being wrong Accept others	Understand "Who" I am Accepting feedback Articulate positions
Norming	Responsibility Contributions	Trust others Respect others' work	Problem sharing Compromise Strategic planning
Performing	Problem sharing Mobilise resources Testing outcomes	Give support to remove complacency	Change process Clarification Resource usage
Mourning	Finalise unfinished business Saying goodbye Following-up	Recognise termination Assert separateness Evaluate outcomes	Unfinished business Affirm and confirm growth

REFLECtION 5.1

Two different sections in a workplace had been combined in order to save costs and encourage professional sharing. While it seemed logical that these areas be combined, probably to the long-term benefit of all concerned, the staff were very anxious about the changes. Letting go of established groups and reforming new ones was a challenge and would take time and energy. Six months later almost everyone was pleased with the change. What might have contributed to this outcome? Think of the five stages of group development in your answer.

Responsibilities and Dynamics

Responsibilities

Having formed a group, and experienced the stages of group development, members of the group develop a sense of groupness that can be characterised by the following elements:

- having a common goal
- working together
- being aware of self
- being motivated to act
- being reliant on one another (interdependence)
- communicating
- being aware of their groupness (entitativity)
- operating within structures and group rules
- being aware of the group's personality (syntality).

Within this set of group characteristics, members are usually very different and thereby bring idiosyncratic beliefs and values that interact with those of others to create a unique working environment. In general, members of the group operate at the level of meeting their own personal needs while realising that a commitment to the group's needs is also required. Activities typically confronted include the desire to initiate activity, seek out and share information, provide opinion, elaborate on a view, coordinate diverse ideas and summarise thoughts on a topic. In respect to supporting the group in its task, individuals help set standards for group performance, encourage other members, accept decisions, express group feelings and operate in a warm and cooperative fashion.

Responsibilities exist for all within a group. However, the role of the group leader is critical to the health and efficient functioning of the group. For many group leaders, 50 to 90% of their working life can be spent within groups that are fundamental to productivity and organisational efficiency. Hence, it is important for leaders to utilise appropriate techniques, particularly in light of the stages of development that groups experience.

Leader Behaviours

Leader behaviours specific to the task and relationship needs of the group at its varying stages can be identified. For instance, leader behaviours that are directive, structured and task oriented are suited to the beginning stages of the group, whereas relationship behaviours that mirror support and democracy appear more beneficial as the group develops. Overall, a balance of leader behaviours is necessary in order to address group needs and recognise stages of group formation.

Apart from exercising prudence in terms of using directive and supportive (task and relationship) influences, the group leader has the primary task of facilitating interactions and managing the speed, depth and the relevance of group debate. In meeting these group goals, the leader has the responsibility of safeguarding the integrity and welfare of group members. The task requires techniques and skills to manage self and others successfully. Skills such as listening, reflecting, structuring, summarising, linking, encouraging, confronting, giving feedback, securing commitment and supporting need to be mastered and used with precision. This need becomes chronically obvious if group members exercise varying levels of understanding and sensitivity to group processes, and/or the issues at hand are controversial and significant.

REFLECtION 5.2

A particular group had been led by a person who was autocratic, non-collaborative and favoured some people over others. As a result of this lack of leadership skills the group had little cohesion and was generally unhappy apart from the favoured few. That leader was replaced, due to illnesss, by a person who was supportive, collaborative, communicative and treated all staff equitably.

What changes do you think might have occurred in the group as a result of leadership change?

Dynamics

Psychological aspects of anxiety, interpersonal sharing and trust become both challenges and imperatives for proper group functioning and associated personal development. Experience confirms a number of operational dynamics that need particular attention if groups are to operate with achievement, hope and credibility. Without deliberate attention to at least these five interrelated areas much of the group's time and energy can be wasted. These significant interrelated areas are authority, individuation, expression, intimacy and work. Questions that need group attention and resolution if the group is to have a clear understanding of its purpose and functioning are shown in Table 5.4.

Table 5.4
Questions to Clarify the Purpose and Function of a Group

Authority
To whom is the group responsible?
How does the group make decisions (voting or consensus)?
Individuality
How was the group constituted (elected or appointed)?
Is membership individual or representational?
Expression
How is information and feeling expressed?
What degree of due process is exercised by the chairperson?
Intimacy
Is openness encouraged?
How do members treat personal data?
Work
Are problem-solving processes used?
To what extent are decisions based on information?

REFLECtION 5.3

We have all been in groups where the dynamics are good and we have unfortunately all been in groups where the dynamics are poor. Try to think of an example you have experienced of each and compare them on the dimensions in Table 5.4.

Group Intervention

The behaviour of a group can be examined in two general areas: (a) how the group is performing as a gathering of individuals operating collectively and (b) whether the tasks of the group are being addressed. Information about the first area can be gleaned by members reflecting on what is constructive about group behaviour, what is proving a problem and what can be planned for

Table 5.5
Ten Occasions for Group Intervention

1. A group member speaks for everyone.
2. An individual speaks for another individual in the group.
3. A group member focuses on persons, conditions or events outside the group.
4. Someone seeks the approval of a group member before and after speaking.
5. Someone says, "I don't want to hurt his/her feelings, so I won't say it".
6. A group member suggests that his/her problems are caused by someone else.
7. An individual suggests, "I've always been that way".
8. An individual suggests, "I'll wait and it will change".
9. Discrepant behaviour appears, for example:
   - between what a member is currently saying and what he/she said earlier
   - between what a member is saying and what she/he is doing
   - between what a member says and what he/she feels
   - between what a member says and what others are feeling in reaction
   - between how a member sees him/herself, and how others see him/her.
10. A member bores the group by rambling.

subsequent meetings to assist the group to operate more effectively. The second area (that pertaining to the achievement of the group's mission) can also be addressed by members recalling their stated group purpose, identifying any apparent gaps between achievements and goals, and addressing these limitations with appropriate strategies. Interventions that may be necessary from time to time are shown in Table 5.5.

Problem Behaviours Within Groups

The most common occurrences in groups that demand attention are those that relate to personal behaviours, which can become distracting to sound interpersonal behaviours. For example, are you familiar with any of the following styles of personal behaviour?

- The Big Noter — "Been there, done that"
- The Know All — "I knew it all anyway"
- The Critic — "Nothing is ever right"
- The Snoozer — "Achieves most outside the meeting"
- The Stoic — "Persists in the light of adversity".

Personalities can become evident in groups and if allowed to "take over" can create disharmony and detract from members having opportunities for balanced input. Some members' behaviours can become non-productive and lead to a concentration of effort and attention to the overall detriment of group relationship development

Table 5.6
Problem Group Behaviours

(i) aggressiveness	⇒	displays of hostility
(ii) blocking	⇒	rejecting ideas without a rationale
(iii) competing	⇒	vying for status and achievement
(iv) seeking sympathy	⇒	attempting to create a personal focus
(v) seeking recognition	⇒	drawing attention to self through unusual behaviour
(vii) withdrawing	⇒	not participating
(viii) pet concerns	⇒	pursuing narrow and subjective interests

and goal achievement. Behaviours that can be a problem for group relationship development are listed in Table 5.6.

These and a host of other unhelpful behaviours can add to group decay and precipitate early termination if not managed appropriately. Intervention can be at the level of the individual or the group as a whole.

For individuals creating difficulties within a group it may be instructive to ask them what their needs are and how can these be met in socially acceptable ways. The challenge for the group leader is to recognise the unique operating styles of individuals and, where problems exist to overall group development, rectify them. A useful technique to support intervention at the individual level is to record some of the more noticeable occurrences of concern and, if found to be applied consistently, then to seek an interview outside of the normal meeting process with the individual concerned. Clarifying for a person their particular mannerisms and the effect this has on the group can help. If the behaviour persists (e.g., repeated interruptions and critical comments without foundation) then correction within the group may be required. In this situation the whole group can lend support to solving the problem.

Intervention with an entire group can follow a problem-solving approach. That is, with the appropriate facilitation, members can be encouraged to reflect on their behaviour as a group and identify any blocking and supporting forces to their productivity and harmony. Action arising from this activity would entail removing blocking forces and retaining those processes that are proving worthwhile. In this way, major alterations to procedures can be avoided and affirmation given to existing practices that have secured clarity, ownership and value. Again, we recommend that regular reviews (perhaps annually) of general group behaviour be undertaken, with the necessary documentation being retained and used as a summary of the group's progress.

REFLECTION 5.4

Have you been in a group where the group leader intervened to make the group more functional? What were some of the issues or behaviours that led to that intervention and how well was it managed? Could you suggest another way it might have been handled?

The Committee: "Why Are we Meeting Like This"?

How often have we heard the following statements about committees? "The camel is a horse designed by committee"; "The best committee is a committee of one"; "Committees keep minutes and waste hours"; "Committees are created by the unable to get the unwilling to do the unnecessary". In spite of all this, organisations still use committees most frequently to find solutions to their challenges. Advantages such as improving information gathering; dividing workload; creating ownership; eliminating hierarchical decision-making; encouraging coordination and cooperation; providing a forum for debate; increasing accuracy of decisions; providing checks and balances on decisions; facilitating acceptance of decisions; providing anonymous solutions to controversial issues; enhancing the administrator's awareness; creating a team attitude; and, increasing professional self-esteem are all suggestive of their contribution to personal, interpersonal and organisational effectiveness.

Committee Roles

Belbin (1981) suggests that within groups individuals take on particular roles and that to be effective, members should recognise, accommodate and utilise these functions to the advantage of the overall group. This is not to suggest that each member plays only one role, but rather individuals may have a preferred or dominant role that is in keeping with their strengths and interests. According to Belbin, the dominant roles usually displayed in teams incorporate eight styles of functioning. These roles are typically demonstrated in problem-solving, coordinative and managerial situations and are quite distinct from particular technical expertise that might be necessary (see Table 5.7).

APPLICATION

Fishbowl Exercise

Task. A staff of eight have to decide on a venue for an end of year gathering.

Process. Each member is required to act out a role in keeping with role limits and associated personality style.

Observation-reflection. The staff will operate in a "fishbowl" format whereby interaction will be observed by others sitting outside the circle and taking notes on the interpersonal interactions taking place.

Preparation. Prior to coming to the meeting a particular role (according to Belbin's terminology) will be allocated to each person and a period of five minutes will be allowed for reflection and visualisation on how the role will be acted out.

The common result of the fishbowl simulation is that individuals usually gain a sound sense of the distinctiveness of the role they have played and whether this matches up with their usual operational style. Moreover, they discover some frustration because of the

Table 5.7
Belbin's Roles and Common Personality Characteristics

Role	Characteristics
Coordinator	calm, self-confident, controlled
Shaper	highly strung, outgoing, dynamic
Completer-Finisher	orderly, conscientious, anxious, painstaking
Implementer	conservative, dutiful, predictable
Monitor-Evaluator	sober, unemotional, prudent
Originator	creative, individualistic, unorthodox
Resource-Investigator	extroverted, enthusiastic, communicative
Supporter	socially oriented, mild, sensitive

inflexible behaviour of some other members and also become increasingly sensitive to the effects that particular roles have on them. Most commonly, simulation participants seek some ideas on the "ideal" group operating style and also look for some creative notions of how to deal with the specific inflexibility of some roles. They also begin to gain a sense of the complementary nature of roles and the synergy that can arise when personality and role are matched and able to operate in an interdependent way.

Adopting an approach to committees that is based on participation, collaboration, shared decision-making and recognition of differences within others creates a particular paradigm for thinking about how we operate collectively in order to achieve personal, group and organisational outcomes. The challenge to functioning in this manner calls not only for a new way of approaching management and group decision-making, but also demands a personal preparedness to "let go" of some of our own orientations, biases and directions. Mary-Benet McKinney (1987) would advocate that such an

Table 5.8
A Shared Wisdom Approach

Implications
  Share our wisdom
  Hear, respect and treasure one another's wisdom
  Work for a climate that is open and respectful

Stances
  Be open to new ways of thinking and feeling
  Be open to information and data collected by others
  Be willing to let go of the need to control
  Be willing to let go of the need to win
  Be willing to let go of the need to always be right
  Be willing to leave the familiar and risk the unfamiliar

Process
  Understand the difference in personality types
  Learn to use the process skills
  Take time for reflection
  Take time to gather the wisdom
  Learn to accept the discerned decision

approach represents a philosophy and commitment to shared wisdom that has implications, stances (actions we must take) and process imperatives. The summaries that are listed in Table 5.8 bring together some of the dominant themes in this chapter and provide a response to the question: why are we meeting like this?

Conclusion

A significant amount of our professional life is spent working with others. This is often formalised in committee or team relationships and calls forth a challenge to give of self, grow personally and develop interpersonally. This chapter has given some attention to the subtlety and complexity of our team, group and committee relationships by exploring some of the stages they go through, the developmental tasks associated with each stage, the dynamics operating within them and some mechanisms for intervention. A model of sharing wisdom has been advocated and the benefits of operating collectively identified.

Chapter 6
Thriving in organisations: contributing to effective workplaces

> It is one of the great ironies of our age that we created organisations to constrain our problematic human natures, and now the only thing that can save these organisations is a full appreciation of the expansive capacity of us humans
> — Margaret Wheatley

Focusing

The Wine Tasters

There were three wine tasters who were confident that they could pick what type of wine they were tasting even if they were blindfolded. Each was blindfolded and taken to a separate room where they were given separate things to do. One was allowed to smell the wine, one was allowed to taste it without smelling it and one was able to take off the blindfold and look at the colour but not taste or smell the wine. Each tried to guess what wine it was. How much more accurate would they have been if all the information was combined?

The story of the wine tasters highlights a central theme to thriving in organisations. Organisations are dynamic places where perceptions and activity constantly interplay as people engage in the "business" of the organisation and at the same time bring to it their experience, skills, relationships and perceptions. Within our organisational context we perform our responsibilities within a microsystem which, while definable, contained and important, exists as part of an overall system. Just as the wine tasters experienced only a part of the wine so do we experience only a part of an organisation, and yet we know there is more to the organisation than we experience.

Key Terms

Culture
Organisational culture is the prevailing background fabric that is manifested in beliefs, values and behaviours associated with the organisation.

System
A system is an organised whole that is made up of interdependent parts, or subsystems, each of which has identifiable boundaries from the overall supra-system.

Rational System
A rational system is an organisation that is identified by an ordered, structured and logical approach to the attainment of goals.

Non-rational System
A non-rational system is an organisation that is characterised by free-flowing, dynamic and natural approaches to meeting system goals.

Imaging
Organisational imaging involves identifying and matching a recognisable image with the dominant characteristics inherent in the organisation.

Concept Development
Ecology of Social Systems

As humans we are influenced and educated through a social need to interact. We do this in a variety of social environments commonly called systems. When we reflect upon the social systems in which we function we come to appreciate the unique nature of our world. Due to the patterns of relationships in our social environment we realise that while social systems at a surface level may appear similar, there is something very unique about each system.
We experience not only the impact from others in our world but also, because of our own level of responsiveness, we create a social reality that is different because of the outcomes we create.

There are at least four levels of systems in society within which we interact. These include the following:
1. personal settings (workplace, peer group, family)
2. the network of personal settings (how personal settings affect each other)
3. the larger system of society (economy, media, government)
4. culture (the pervasive ethos of values, beliefs and standards that defines our socialisation).

In system terms, what becomes important to observe are the behaviours that emerge as a consequence of the dynamic interaction among all the parts of the system. For example, within the social system of the classroom, what needs and wants exist among class members? How do such things as class goals affect student relationships? What impact do incentives have? How is power wielded? Are student working conditions of a satisfactory standard?
How has the tradition of the school influenced reward systems? Through seeking the answers to such questions, the system of the class can begin to take on a new perspective and the students within it observed in a different light. The system comes alive and has

an ecology, which when understood, is seen as a significant influence on the life of each student.

Development within family life is another example where the importance of social systems is recognisable. Remember that the family has relationships with other systems (extended family, work, community, neighbourhood, etc.), but within itself has specific elements that interact and influence each individual's growth. In other words, as changes occur within the system this creates a ripple effect that influences the overall harmony among those making up the system. For example, a child's relationship with a parent is not merely dependent upon a two-way interaction, but rather influenced by the pattern of relationships within which both individuals are found at any point in time.

REFLECTION 6.1

What are the important features that operate within your family system? What are the internal and external factors that have the greatest effect on your system?

Mapping Organisational Systems

The challenge to understand and intervene in the social systems that engulf our lives can also be applied to the organisations in which we work. The goal of enriching these places in order to make our activities valuable, dignified and personally rewarding becomes part of thriving in organisations and ensuring that they are growth producing and not growth inhibiting.

The design of an organisation is seen in its component elements. These elements are those that constitute the essential parts of any organisation and can be identified as being part of at least four interactive subsystems. These include (a) business purpose, which is inclusive of strategic and operational elements; (b) human resources, which involves people and relationship functions; (c) culture, which incorporates tangible and intangible elements; and (d) administration, which involves the exercising of leadership and management. Each of these subsystems has a number of subparts that contribute to a dynamic interplay within the overall organisation.

Business Purpose

The business purpose of an organisation involves its strategic direction and the associated operational elements forming part of the day-to-day functioning of the enterprise.

The *strategic* elements include the following:
- environment: services, products, regulations and technology that offer opportunity or threat
- mission: the overall purpose of the business
- clients: those to receive a service or for whom a product is developed
- policies: authoritative statements applied to particular areas of the organisation's mission
- values: an integrated set of values or guidelines that govern business practice
- functions: the major categories of service or products offered to clients
- key result areas: particular areas of achievement within each of the core functions
- strategic plan: integration of the above into long-term directions and aims for the organisation.

The *operational* elements include the following:
- aims: areas of accomplishment within key result areas
- objectives: specific targets to be achieved within programs
- programs: activities to achieve objectives

- non-people resources: material resources necessary to achieve program objectives
- performance plan: annual operational priorities for specific activities that interconnect with the overall strategy of the organisation.

Human Resources

The achievement of the business purpose of the organisation involves the way in which an organisation uses its human resources to deliver its services or develop its products. Human resource organisational elements include the joint aspects of personnel and the nature of relationships among people in the workplace.

Personnel elements include the following:
- roles and responsibilities: identification and documentation of the nature, coverage and allocation of tasks
- reward systems: incentives to support performance
- individual performance plans: the means by which individuals link particular activities with broader organisational objectives.

Relationships elements include the following:
- teamwork: the nature and extent of cooperation between individuals and groupings of personnel
- communication: the extent and nature of effective information sharing
- corporate unity: the ability of individuals to work knowingly about the overall organisational objectives.

Culture

The generation of services and products will inevitably create a culture within the organisation and impact on its purpose and human resource capacity. Culture pervades all aspects of an organisation and is manifested in tangible features as well as those characteristics that are intangible but significant to the effectiveness and efficiency of an organisation.

Tangible elements include the following:
- quality of life: the legitimate needs of personnel within the organisation
- traditions and procedures: the time-honoured practices that have become institutionalised
- uniforms, symbols and icons: representations of dress codes, beliefs and values common across the organisation
- ceremonies, rituals and language: behavioural activities that celebrate and reinforce core aspects of organisational life.

Intangible elements include the following:
- individual differences: the extent to which difference and idiosyncrasy is accommodated
- affect: the impact to an organisation based on employee security, belonging, prestige and self-fulfilment
- social: the organisation's social system, which includes relationships, group cohesion and personality
- unexpected forces: happenings that are unsystematic and unplanned but influence functioning
- politics: the distribution of power and influence in an organisation.

Administration

The term administration applies to those people who are formally appointed to lead and manage the organisation. Leadership involves the development and facilitation of vision and direction, whereas management incorporates the design and implementation of planning systems to achieve desired outcomes.

Leadership systems include the following:
- vision formulation: formulating policy, regulations, procedures and guidelines
- vision and implementation: applying the vision to ordinary day-to-day happenings of the organisation

- vision communication: sharing the vision throughout the organisation to promote cohesion and conviction
- vision and structure: ensuring that the structures and processes of the organisation provide a clear reflection of the vision
- vision and decision: making decisions in the light of the organisation's vision
- vision and celebration: supporting the organisation in celebrating the vision in ritual form.

Management systems include the following:
- planning: setting goals and making decisions for implementation
- administration: operating for organisational efficiency
- industrial: establishing conditions in the workplace
- information and communication technology: introducing management information systems
- personnel: selecting, inducting, training and reviewing people to participate appropriately
- finance: allocating and accounting for resources.

The mapping of an organisation's component elements assists in understanding its complexity and the areas within which its overall performance can be examined.

REFLECtION 6.2

Think about a large organisation in which you have worked. Look at each subheading of the section above and think about how your organisation operated. What are three key improvements you could recommend for your organisation?

Dynamic Systems

The experience of watching a game of "live" cricket is worlds apart from looking at a picture of figures standing lifeless on the cover of a glossy cricket magazine. Similarly, to observe an organisation only from the perspective of those elements that constitute it is to lose much of what actually comprises the dynamics that give the organisation its character and personality. Organisations are much more than composite pictures of administration, business purpose, human relations and cultural elements. They are living, breathing enterprises.

The experience of organisational life is seldom defined by any one of the subsystems operating independently from other subsystems, or existing in isolation from external forces. Rather, an organisation is best depicted as a living and dynamic entity, constituted by numerous subsystems, and exposed to influences (within and without) on its areas of service at any point in time. Because of this, the overriding nature of the organisation will be dynamic and adaptive as it renews continuously in the context of influences that are seen and unseen, predicted and unpredicted, managed and unmanaged.

The dynamism of an organisation is also influenced by the degree to which it is able to interact with other similar organisations and organisations within the community as a whole. A closed organisation is self-contained and independent, perhaps even isolated from the community within which it exists. Such an organisation may well focus on its purpose, yet, because of the limited engagement elsewhere, it may suffer from absence of feedback and loss of opportunity for improvement. Alternatively, an open organisation recognises the need to interact with the environment. Characteristics of an open system include a recognition of its interdependence with the environment, a flow of energy between the two, a search for constant feedback on service and the engagement of continuing improvement. While an open system is in a position to grow through being attentive and responsive to the greater whole, it is also important to ensure that the quality of its internal processes are not reduced. The essence would therefore reside in balancing internal maintenance in the light of adaptation to the outside world.

While it is arguable that every organisational system is dynamic and different, each one can be identified in terms of its rational and non-rational constitutive parts. The rational elements are those aspects of its practice that are consistent, tangible and observable, whereas the non-rational elements include aspects of a less concrete nature, usually difficult to measure and more in the domain of the relational and intuitive. The non-rational elements of information, relationships and identity, and the rational components of structure, process and policy, combine and interact to give the organisation direction. Notwithstanding the significance of the rational elements, non-rational aspects of the organisation hold the most power to achieve its purposes.

REFLECtION 6.3

How would you describe the dynamic character of an organisation you have experienced? Why have you chosen to describe the organisation in this way?

Releasing the Spirit in Organisations

It is repeatedly stated that the power of an organisation rests with those who comprise it: its people. However, the emphasis on people is often from the perspective of consumer needs, or the impact on service as a consequence of interaction and relationships. Central to these perspectives is the belief that clients are important, and hence the focus on "doing for" or being "directive about" how people might be treated has become the norm. The approach manifests a "top down" orientation where those who are "supposed to know" act in ways that are directive and controlling, and those who are "supposed to act" do just that. Even though the client might be the focus, control in this form of organisational thinking rests with a few, and similarly, full responsibility is located primarily with those in management positions.

A new and exciting direction in organisational thinking would be to alter the balance of control and responsibility within organisations in a way that addressed staff members' unique abilities and respected their innate sense of responsibility and motivation towards improvement. In such a model, directive and controlling mechanisms would give way to the provision of freedom, and, in turn, freedom would advance self-regulation and increase responsibility. The model is built on the belief that organisations are essentially living systems, where the non-rational elements of the organisation are at the core of its success. Organisations of this kind would attend to the power of the spirit in people and unleash their capacity to act creatively and responsibly. Successful organisations of the future should be more attentive to the spirit of their people, as it is through the dynamic and vibrant enterprise of the spirit that organisations will have most chance of achieving desired outcomes.

REFLECTION 6.4

How would recognition of the spirit impact on your organisation. What difference would it make to the way people were managed within it?

Organisational Culture

Culture pervades all aspects of an organisation. It is the oxygen that breathes life into the operations of a system; it is what gives the organisation its meaning. Its principal elements comprise beliefs and values that are commonly expressed in the vision and mission. Culture is not restricted to individual perception, nor is it arrived at easily. It is generated over time, expressed in symbol and ritualistic behaviours and is used continually as the basis for all happenings and negotiations within the organisation's life.

Culture captures an organisation's foundations and what it values as worthwhile for its future. The culture of an organisation therefore binds and gives colour to everything it does; it is the "stated and unstated" that serves to clarify what may be vague or ambiguous to the person outside the organisation. Culture gives the organisation meaning and purpose.

REFLECtION 6.5

Has a culture developed within your organisation? If so, how is it manifested? Does it clarify the meaning of the organisation? Table 6.1 may help your reflection.

Organisational Images

Representing the complexity of an organisation's everyday life in metaphorical terms may be achieved by considering organisations as being either rational or non-rational. Typical of the rational model is the formation of a bureaucracy. In its extreme it is an organisation governed solely by rules and regulations — a place where inspection and evaluation breed compliance and where rigid structures exist to

Table 6.1
Culture Within Organisations

Verbal	Visual	Behavioural
Aims	Crests	Ceremonies
Goals	Mottos	Language
Objectives	Uniforms	Structures
Traditions	Symbols	Procedures
Legends	Icons	Rituals

ensure goals are achieved. Alternatively, non-rational or "natural" organisations are more loosely configured with elements of change, flexibility and ambiguity being found in observable behaviour.

The school as organisation, for example, could be seen as comprising both rational and non-rational elements, with an emphasis on cultural and symbolic features providing the links (between the elements). At the heart of the organisation would be the cultural myth out of which would emerge its beliefs, mission, policies, programs, resources, organisation and day-to-day operations. These elements would constantly interact and serve to alter the balance of influence that any particular element would possess. The rational aspects of this model (e.g., goals, school regulations, instructional timetable) would be enshrined along with elements of the non-rational (e.g., flexibility in instructional approaches, changing priorities in goal attainment, variable assessment practices).

The contrast between rational and non-rational systems and the desirability of incorporating elements of both parallels the "hard" and "soft" administrative practices that exist in schools. The hard elements would be those bureaucratic requirements that possess logical analysis, quantification and perhaps impersonality, whereas the soft dimensions would entail the human aspects of needs, values and people's dispositions. The metaphors of boxes and bubbles illustrate how the hard and soft aspects of schools can be characterised. What provides the connectedness between the hard facts and soft processes are the bonds — the shared understanding and meaning of the culture in which the boxes and bubbles can exist. The bonds provide the common purpose and shared vision out of which emerge the supportive relationships that in turn reinforce the bonds and create community.

REFLECTION 6.6

Develop an image that reflects your organisation best. Why did you choose this image? How do you think it might be perceived by others?

APPLICATION

Perspectives on Culture

The life of an organisation can be examined from a variety of perspectives. The first perspective is cognitive. Looking through this lens we are challenged to look at an organisation from the viewpoint of what it believes, what members think about the way it goes about its mission and what knowledge exists and is shared. What is the cognitive culture like in your organisation?

A second perspective on culture is symbolic. To what extent do shared symbols or rituals characterise its life and provide meaning about what is valued? How do experiences become interpreted in this symbolic way and how does this provide a sense of satisfaction or frame of reference?

The third perspective is psychodynamic; that is, how does the culture of an organisation give expression to an individual's unconscious psychological processes, such as the need for belonging, security, care, prestige, self-fulfilment and so on?

Considering organisational culture through cognitive, symbolic and psychodynamic perspectives helps us to identify and understand the prevailing culture. This understanding of culture then provides particular benefits and ensures survival and growth rather than feelings of oppression and limited worth. Understanding culture is therefore significant to our growth interpersonally because it:

- assists our awareness of how the current situation arose
- suggests courses of action that are preferable
- allows for "fine tuning" of action
- provides a means for anticipating consequences

- establishes a framework for long-term strategic planning.

Reflecting on organisational culture allows us to share perceptions, interpret events and transform ourselves, group and larger organisational membership into some constructive action. Understanding culture will assist this transformation, because if we work within cultural limits we will receive more support than opposition and provide for survival and enrichment rather than difficulty and decay. Imaging organisational culture is an important further step.

Imaging Organisations

Six images of an organisation are summarised below:

1. Organisation as machine: An organisation made up of inter-locking parts, with each part playing a clearly defined role oriented to success and a mode of operation that is efficient.
2. Organisation as political system: an organisation as a system of government drawing on political principles to legitimate rules and factors that shape political life (staying in power).
3. Organisation as organism: an organisation consisting of interrelated subsystems that will grow, develop, decline and eventually die in a natural environment.
4. Organisation as culture: an organisation based on shared meaning sustained by values, beliefs, rituals and norms bound together by culture.
5. Organisation as relationships: an organisation dominated by relationships where individuals work collaboratively for communal and individual growth.
6. Organisation as brain: an organisation focused on intelligent strategies to define progress and overcome problems.

The organisation in which you work may not be categorised easily by reference to one of the images and nor should it be. The images are a series of options for consideration. As no one description may fit your own organisational perceptions, there could be elements of each that provide relevance and meaning. The following questions may assist you to focus.

1. What processes are used in my organisation to achieve our mission?

   ....

2. Which process management principles characterise how and why decisions occur?

   ....

3. With these responses in mind, my image of organisational life is predominantly:

   ....

Conclusion

Thriving in an organisation is dependent on understanding and contributing constructively to its culture. Organisational life is complex and so too are the skills necessary if the individual is to grow within the social system that occupies and defines so much of working life. Personal skills involve recognising the complexity of your subsystem and the dynamics that apply. Central to making a positive impact is the ability to see your place and significance in the organisation and so utilise your spirit for growth.

Chapter 7
Everyone is a Leader: Facilitating Interpersonal Development

> The wicked leader is he who people despise.
> The good leader is he who people revere.
> The great leader is he who people say,
> we did it ourselves.
> — Lao Tsu

Focusing

A Vision for the Future

A sports goods company sponsored a team of four professional tennis players who toured the international circuit for some years, gradually growing in reputation and confidence but becoming increasingly aware of the demands that competition at the top level was placing on them. The sponsoring company decided that the players needed an official team captain to take responsibility for their leadership and direction, but was unsure about which player to select. The company asked a well-known tennis coach to interview the four and make a recommendation. The first player advised that the team was functioning well and saw no reason for one player to be nominated as their leader. The second player supported the concept of a captain who would ensure stricter team discipline in terms of practice hours, rest times and diet. The third suggested additional coaching to improve certain aspects of their play. The fourth player recommended that all four should leave the circuit for six months of intensive coaching, thereby losing their appearance money but endeavouring to improve their competitiveness and success in the long term. The coach recommended the fourth player as team leader.

The parable of the tennis coach and his choice of a team leader shows us something of the essence of leadership — *vision*. With a vision, the leader has an appreciation of the future, can act with intention and clarity, and can assess progress by way of clearly established milestones. Vision gives direction and goals. It can be used in our personal and professional lives and can provide life and energy. It need not necessarily be in terms of status or authority; it can be expressed in lifestyle, values or personal skills and behaviours. For example, a teacher's vision may not be to aspire to the position of principal but rather to stages of effective teaching and meaningful appreciation and management of students. Alternatively, a vision for a young executive might be to achieve management excellence, while for a secretary, vision may entail the development and mastery of the technical skills associated with office responsibilities. Whatever the goal, vision provides the glimpse of a future that is valued and for which effort may be expended to ensure its accomplishment.

The volume of literature on leadership is frightening. Because of its expansiveness and complexity, it is arguably one of the most difficult areas from which to draw personal meaning. Leadership is a field that is also easily ignored because so many people do not perceive themselves as leaders and therefore possess no direct interest in the subject. However, as the chapter title suggests "everyone is a leader" and there is "room at the top for everyone". Bearing this in mind, how can we all be leaders and what are the challenges facing us?

Key Terms

Vision
Vision is a view of the future; an expression of a desirable state to move towards.

Leadership
Leadership is the exercise of influence through relationships. This is exercised by all within the community (common leadership) and expected of those in administrative positions (administrative leadership).

Theory X and Theory Y
Theory X expresses a pessimistic view of "subordinates". Theory Y presumes an optimistic view of "subordinates".

Self-fulfilling Prophecy
Self-fulfilling prophecy is the powerful and directive effect of expectations on people's behaviour.

Concept Development
Types of Leadership

A leader is someone who is able to enhance the life of a group by exercising an influence on decision-making through their actions, words, collaborative activity and vision. A leader, therefore, can make a difference and can exercise power by participating and being creative. This conceptualisation of leadership, however, has not been a persistent theme in social science literature, nor has it been evident in organisational life where management is described or lived out in "leader" and "follower" terms.

Distributive-common Leadership
A common perception about leadership is that it involves only a few people within the organisation, usually those who hold administrative positions, those who possess authority, or perhaps the people who participate actively on committees or boards connected with the organisation. This understanding, while possessing some face validity, is counter to what experience teaches. Those individuals whose activities reflect the organisation's mission and advance its reputation are often not who are expected. The reality is that all

individuals within the organisation play an important role, because it is through teamwork and interdependence that the organisation's goals are achieved.

Professor Frank Crowther, a principal researcher on leadership best practice, describes leadership that embraces all within the educational community, particularly teachers, as parallel leadership (Crowther, 1999). His research demonstrates that teachers are significant to change within schools and that the processes that teachers use are not dissimilar from those that have been traditionally attributed to management personnel (principals). Commenting two years after the initial investigations into the impact of parallel leadership, Crowther (2001, p. 4) drew three conclusions with confidence: "educational leadership is alive and well in the teaching profession and is not restricted to the school administration; parallel leadership describes this phenomenon; teacher leadership can be nurtured, but requires a complex range of administrator capabilities".

The essence of parallel leadership is that it entails processes that "ordinary people do extraordinarily". Leadership behaviours of a parallel nature are, however, not expressed uniquely. Those people who are able to achieve real and lasting change appear to behave in consistent ways. The model also reinforces the position that the potential for change and influence resides with every person within the organisational environment. With such an emphasis, the model summarises at a theoretical level what has been thought intuitively about leadership in educational settings for a long time. In a similar way, personnel within organisations that have a strong focus on client services clearly play a critical leadership role in service delivery and organisational improvement.

REFLECTION 7.1

Reflect on an example of parallel leadership that you know of that has worked well? What factors contributed to its success?

Administrative Leadership

Notwithstanding the leadership potential of all within an organisational community, a generally held view is that leadership is one of the key responsibilities for those who hold administrative positions. What constitutes this particular sort of leadership and does it have any bearing on the leadership that is common to all?

The breadth of leadership responsibilities and associated competencies is great. The four generic domains of responsibility — self, relationships, management systems and organisational operations — are an illustration of this. The expected outcomes, or key result areas, within each generic domain detail the breadth of responsibility included in each field (see Table 7.1). What is significant about the framework is the breadth of leadership influence, and the power of being present with, to and for others that is apparent within the life of the organisation.

The leadership domains identified for those who are in administrative positions also underpin leadership influence by others within the organisation. Every person seeking to be an effective leader is required to possess an understanding of self, relationships, management systems and organisational operations. While levels of sophistication in these domains will vary in accordance with experience, role, training and qualifications, some accomplishment in each of these fields is a powerful prerequisite for the practice of leadership influence.

The successful performance of any form of leadership responsibilities (parallel or administrative) in contemporary organisational settings assumes the application of knowledge, skills and

Table 7.1
Leadership Domains and Their Key Result Areas

Leadership Domain	Key Result Area (Management Speak)	Interpretation
Self	Belief, vision, mission	What do I value most? What is my vision for my life?
	Self-concept and self-esteem	How do I think of myself and value myself?
	Role clarification	What is my job in the various areas of my life?
	Task priority and delivery	What do I do, in what sequence, and how do I do it?
	Professional support	Who supports me and whom do I support?
	Accountability relationships	Who am I responsible to, and for what? Who is responsible to me?
Relationships	Communication	How well do I let my needs and opinions be known? How well do I understand the needs and opinions of others?
	Group formation and functioning	Forming working relationships and maintaining them.
	Empowerment of others	Encouraging, nurturing and facilitating the skills of others.
	Responsibility	Sometimes we lead and supervise. Sometimes we are led and are supervised.
Management Systems	Resource acquisition	Earning money.
	Finance management	Deciding how you spend your money.
	Information technology	Using technology as a management tool.
	Human resources	Selecting, supporting and evaluating people.
	Industrial relationships	Applying just and acceptable workplace practices.
Organisational Operations	Design and structure	How is the workplace organised?
	Renewal and development	The system is growing and developing.

Table 7.1 Continued

Leadership Domain	Key Result Area (Management Speak)	Interpretation
	Community engagement	The system has to interact with the outside world.
	Policy development	Articulating what is important for this system.
	Futures orientation	Thinking ahead and being prepared.
	Accountability	Being responsible for our decisions and actions.

behaviours. The knowledge competency covers the technical information necessary to perform a leadership role, the skills competency identifies the abilities central to the carriage of responsibilities, and the behaviours competency indicates the observable behaviours that the leader demonstrates. When these competencies are applied to the four generic areas of leadership responsibility (self, relationships, management systems and organisational operations) the potential for leadership influence takes on a pervasive and profound nature (see Table 7.2). Leadership becomes central to the whole of life. It aligns with self, is expressed through relationships, exists in management systems and is an important part of overall organisational functioning. It possesses a consistent spirit and is expressed and developed in a dynamic and adaptive fashion.

REFLECtiON _____ 7.2

What administrative leadership competencies do you possess? What skills do you need to work on to improve your performance in this area?

Table 7.2
Competencies Required for Leadership Responsibilities

Leadership Domain	Skills	Behaviours
Self	Reflection Commitment Time management Prioritising Reporting	Imaging Symbolising Celebrating Renewing
Relationships	Motivating Cooperating Sharing wisdom Networking Counselling Mediating Problem-solving Conflict-resolving	Serving Teaming Assessing Aligning Affirming Empowering Challenging Collaborating
Management Systems	Team establishment Team selection Team induction Team development Performance review	Analysing Unifying Reviewing Negotiating Developing
Organisational Operations	Promotion Strategic planning Policy writing Accountability Reporting	Representing Advocating Policy facilitating Story telling Learning

Leadership Style

Implementing leadership that is visionary and participative demands a view of organisations and their people that is based on empowerment, interdependence and trust. It is the belief that we cannot work together if we don't value the contributions of others, give them opportunities to perform and trust them to work effectively and efficiently. In other words, this form of leadership behaviour is very reliant upon how people are viewed and how they are valued.

Douglas McGregor (1960, as cited in Hersey & Blanchard, 1977) commented on the impact of valuing others and its effect on leadership four decades ago. The theory is still significant because it demonstrates that while a leader may have a vision, a vision alone is not enough. Not only is a vision for the future a prerequisite for leadership, but also a leader needs to possess appropriate attitudes about colleagues if such a vision is to be implemented with confidence and support.

McGregor argued that leaders in organisations held assumptions about their colleagues ("followers" in his terminology) that were either negative (Theory X) or positive (Theory Y). In Theory X people possess limited ambition, are reluctant to work and avoid responsibility. Management therefore needs to motivate, organise, control and coerce workers in order to achieve the organisation's objectives. Alternatively, in Theory Y people are motivated by needs, and if these can be addressed then motivation is enhanced.
In this latter theory, people have a desire to grow and to be self-directed, motivated and responsible.

McGregor's work is important because it shows that our attitudes or assumptions about others affect how we behave towards them. A leader who holds negative views about colleagues is likely to act in a way that conveys such a belief. This in turn can create a self-fulfilling prophecy that reinforces the negative belief to a deeper level. Alternatively, positive beliefs about co-workers can create an environment that breeds growth and development and is itself

Table 7.3
A Continuum of Leader Behaviours

Leader-Centred Behaviours			to		Group-Centred Behaviours	
Leader decides announces decision	Leader decides sells decision	Leader presents ideas invites questions	Leader presents tentative idea subject to group	Leader presents alternatives group decides	Leader defines boundaries group decides	Group defines boundaries and decides

optimistic. Workers' behaviour would reinforce this optimism and give credibility to it. Expectations can therefore precipitate outcomes.

To summarise McGregor's work is to say that our leadership styles, the way we operate with others in the achievement of our vision, are closely related to our understanding of self and others. Of course leadership styles are seldom so definite that we can say that an individual's style is categorically "this or that", because behaviour often varies with situations. Because of this, it is better to think of leadership styles as varying along a continuum from leader-centred (autocratic) to group-centred (democratic). At one extreme the leader decides everything, while at the other, the leader is a member of the group that, on the whole, makes decisions collectively. In this latter situation the relevant "authority" provides authority to the consensus arising within the group's observations.

The range of possible leadership behaviours is presented by Tannenbaum, Weschler and Massarik (1961) in their treatment of the relationship between individual and group leadership. They distinguished between "boss-centred leadership" and "subordinate-centred leadership" and identified the nature of decision-making, depending on the levels of significance given to "boss" or "subordinates". As shown in Table 7.3, the level of involvement of the group varies as the extent of singular leader influence changes.

The manifestation of leader behaviour in terms of a predominant style can be observed and reflects experience, basic beliefs and values about self and others. The complex nature of leadership becomes evident, and if we are to assume that the most effective leadership comes from giving others emancipation in terms of influencing decisions, particular skills are needed. Along with vision, the leader and the group need to be reflective and collegial in their approach. They are challenged to be prophetic in terms of their vision and "grounded" in so far as they recognise what is real and important for the group. Above all, they must be dynamic and flexible in their approach.

REFLECTION 7.3

Are certain styles of leadership associated with specific types of organisations? Does a person with various leadership characteristics become a good leader anywhere?

I once knew an army officer who had held a very high rank in the armed services before leaving to take up a position as manager of a tourist resort. He was suffering from severe stress despite the fact that the tourist resort had a much smaller staff than what he had been responsible for in the army. He also had quite a good knowledge of the tourist industry and could not understand why he was having difficulty coping.

How could this highly successful and proven leader have difficulty coping in this new situation? What would you do to alter the situation?

APPLICATION

Leadership Myths

This chapter opened with the declaration that the literature on leadership was voluminous, changing, and by implication, easily misunderstood. This is often observed in the practice of leadership and in discussions about appropriate styles of leadership. The dominant theme of this paper, however, has been that leadership involves vision, which can be practised by everyone.

Timm, Peterson and Stephens (1990, p. 134) suggest that it would be useful to "puncture" the myths that permeate the whole subject of leadership. In doing this they contrast the reality of people's lives with mythical, often heard statements about leadership that are not congruent with practice.

The exercise that follows expresses some of the myths about leadership and contrasts these with reality statements. Reflect on each of the myths and add your own comments from experience that support the belief that the statement is, in fact, a myth. (A myth is a traditional belief that may be widely accepted but not verifiable from practice.)

Myth 1 — Leadership is a Rare Skill
Reality:
- Everyone has leadership potential.
- People may be leaders in one organisation and followers in another.
- Leadership opportunities are plentiful and within the reach of most people.

Myth 2 — Leaders are Born, not Made
Reality:
- Leadership is not a gift of grace too abstract to be defined.
- The title of the leader is often misunderstood because it is attributed to those whose actions take place in the most dramatic realms of human endeavour (e.g., Mahatma Ghandi, Napoleon, Winston Churchill).
- This myth limits the areas, ways and situations in which leadership can occur.

Myth 3 — Leaders Are Created by Extraordinary Circumstances
Reality:
- This myth limits the opportunities for leadership because it indicates that leadership is only associated with some sort of grand cataclysm or rise and fall of power; we have no opportunity to exercise leadership skills under normal circumstances.

Myth 4 — Leadership Exists only at the Top of an Organisation
Reality:
- We feed this myth by focusing on top leadership when many corporations have thousands of leadership roles available to employees.
- Leadership is needed in every single unit, at every level of the organisation.

Myth 5 — The Leader Controls, Directs, Prods, Manipulates
Reality:
- Leadership is not so much the exercise of power but the ability to empower others.
- Leaders align their energies with others; they pull rather than push, and inspire rather than command.
- Rewards and punishments maintain control through intimidation; a leader's tools are very different.

Myth 6 — Leaders Are Charismatic
Reality:
- Some are, most are not.
- There are always a few leaders who correspond to our fantasies of "divine inspiration" and "grace under pressure" (e.g., John F. Kennedy), but most leaders are all too human — fallible, flawed, with no particular charm that separates them externally from their followers.
- Charisma is the result of effective leadership, not the other way around.

Myth 7 — It Is Immoral to Seek Power
Reality:
- Power is associated with those who abuse and misuse it rather than those who use it wisely.
- We confuse power with subjugation and control; in doing so, we reject power, whether consciously or unconsciously, and thereby restrict our own opportunities for leadership.
- Power is energy, and as with any form of energy its value lies in how we use it. Until utilised, power is neutral. It is neither benign nor corrupt.

Visualising Leadership

A consistent approach in this book has been the use of images to create meaning and facilitate change. Tom Sergiovanni (1987) would advance that images are a form of "mindscape", which provides a new perspective on reality. Therefore, we would like you, in this section, to reflect on your image of leadership (your mindscape) and share it with others. You need not restrict it to a visual image;

perhaps personalities from literature or theatre, for example, better create for you that strength of conviction that gives meaning, provides energy and leads to action.

An image used by David Hunt in his text *The Renewal of Personal Energy* (1992) speaks to us about leadership. It captures a reality in which we experience diversity but also giftedness. It allows for us all to be leaders and it challenges us to respect the dignity and contribution that all our colleagues bring to a learning, productive and growing organisation. We hope you too can identify with this image. It is not our own creation, but as we experienced it for the first time we were able to identify with it, becoming captured by its richness and power to convey a message.

REFLECTION 7.4

Balloons

My image is of myself holding a bouquet of multi-coloured balloons. These balloons are unlike other balloons. They are not filled with air but rather with my developed and underdeveloped qualities. Some of the balloons are large (my developed qualities) and have long strings so they soar above the others. Other balloons are small (my underdeveloped qualities) with shorter strings so they tend to bob below the larger ones. Other people around me are also holding balloons of various sizes on varying lengths of string. The fun part comes in sharing balloons because it gives my smaller balloons a boost and helps them soar a little higher (Hunt, 1992, p. 56).

Take time to reflect on your images of leadership. What recollections speak to you? What is it about them that brings them to mind? And how can they be used to foster a new image towards your understanding of leadership?

Conclusion

Possession of a vision is central to leadership, but so too are the skills and behaviours to make the vision reality. While we must begin with vision, vision alone is not enough. Allied with our vision for where we might like to take our personal and professional lives are the processes we use and our appreciation of others within these processes. In this chapter we have argued for leadership to be group centred and based on relationships. We have suggested that our views about self and others influence how we operate with others and argued that by being imaginative, working with reality and being reflective, we can be dynamic; that is, we can change, grow and lead in relationships through the use of well-developed people skills.

Chapter 8
Keeping on, keeping on: sustaining interpersonal development through renewal

> We shall not cease from exploration
> and the end of all our exploring
> will be to arrive where we started
> and know the place for the first time
> — T.S. Eliot

Focusing

> We trained hard ... but it seemed that every time we were beginning to form up into teams we would be reorganised ... I was to learn later in life that we tend to meet any new situation by reorganising; and a wonderful method it can be for creating the illusion of progress while producing confusion, inefficiency and demoralisation (Petronious, 210 BC).

The statement by Petronious starkly reminds us of the universal principle of change — it will always be with us. As we journey through life our unique personalities, attitudes, skills and values will unfold and take shape. Moreover, as we function within systems (both social and organisational) that are themselves in varying states of growth, we will be further challenged to adjust, change and renew. The consequences of this can be detrimental if we are not equipped to understand and utilise our experience as opportunity and draw from our basic values to sustain our adjustments.

Key Terms

Renewal
Renewal involves returning to core values and making adjustments in keeping with these values.

Renewal Stages
Renewal stages are a set of process steps that typically underpin the exercise of renewal.

Renewal Principles
These are directional principles that orientate an individual or organisation towards renewal.

Life-world
The life-world is the world of our own relationships, practicalities, dreams, hopes and reality.

System-world
The system-world is the world of regulation, order, procedure, accountability and expectation that is imposed upon us.

Co-creation
A process of sharing that goes beyond mere "show and tell" to a level where a special relationship exists that permits the release of energy to re-create and renew what is shared.

Renewal and its Context

The first point to make about renewal is to stress what it is not. It is not equal to change. Certainly, change is part of renewal, but only in so far as observable differences may exist in an action or structure that has emerged from renewal. Change only states the obvious, renewal gives the reason and provides the example. An illustration of change might be a person who has undergone substantial weight loss, developed healthier eating habits and a more balanced lifestyle. To say this person has changed would be correct, but to indicate that such change was based on a return to a new set of values that underpinned these changes is to articulate renewal. Renewal is essentially a within-self dimension that facilitates continuing change on the basis of what individuals or groups actually want to achieve (Hunt, 1987, 1991).

Renewal and renewing activities do not exist in a vacuum. They are influenced by personal (subjective) and impersonal (objective) factors that contextualise and compound its nature. Recognising the interaction between these multiple factors, Jurgen Habermas (1984a, 1984b) conceptualised the modern world as being represented by the life of the individual (the life-world) and the life around the individual that provides some guidelines for operation (the system-world). According to Habermas, the life-world is an environment where cultural traditions, group cohesiveness, personal identity, values and relationships are significant and thereby sustained and reproduced. Conversely, the elements of the system-world, which include the powerful forces of norms, regulations, compliance and accountability, are more objective and quantitative. These two worlds need to be held in a creative tension, because if one dominates or "colonises" the other, an imbalance occurs. Life-world considerations need always to be checked against objective system-world norms, while system-world initiatives need to be clarified in the life-world to ensure that they are appropriate.

If renewal is to occur successfully at either the personal or organisational level, life-world and system-world influences should be considered. Individuals who want to change their lifestyles must not only consider subjective issues, but also be conscious of the impact of the objective pressures and requirements impacting on their existence. Such an approach, while seemingly obvious, can too often be ignored in the frenzy to introduce a new desired state.

A powerful force for bringing the life-world and system-world together suggested by Habermas (1984a, 1984b) is communicative action, which seeks to identify the implications for renewal in both domains. What becomes important in this sharing is not only the testing of the realistic chances of renewal ideas or programs, but also the development of relationships and shared meaning that come as a consequence of these exchanges.

REFLECTION 8.1

A close friend recently resigned from his position as a senior executive in a huge multinational corporation. Everyone was very surprised because he was highly paid and destined for great career success. He explained that his family had always come first in his life and his job was now taking almost all of his time from the family. He had realised this a few months before he resigned and had decided to adjust his professional lifestyle in keeping with this value system. Without doubt it was clear that the system-world and life-world within which he operated required that he feed and clothe his family as well as spend time with them. For this reason he undertook a process of renewal to consider his next employment position, which would enable him to spend time with his family but also to care for them appropriately.

Look at your life-world and system-world pressures that affect your ability to renew.

Renewal as Co-creation

Renewal is a discovery, usually in association or with the help of others, of what is valued and the determination of processes and actions towards making concrete these fundamental values. In other words, irrespective of whether renewal is at the personal

or organisational level, the challenge to renew is premised upon three fundamental and foundational requirements:
- the need to identify core values, mission and goals (the vision)
- the need to determine the stages that may lead to the accomplishment of the vision
- the need to generate basic management principles that will provide guidance in the process.

Identifying Core Values, Mission and Goals (Vision)

Sharing ideas can be energy evoking and, if used wisely, can become creative. When two people share their thoughts there is not only a release of energy, but also a number of advantages emerge. These include the following:

1. enlisting emotional support from people who listen, understand and accept
2. promoting confidence because of the affirmation given to a view
3. Increasing understanding through deepening personal reflections
4. offering new perspectives by advancing new ways of thinking and viewing situations
5. releasing energy by igniting motivation and thought
6. providing a basis for planning action through brainstorming possibilities and checking them with another person.

Sharing values is not necessarily the same process as communicative action, but there are similarities that can be drawn. The two activities are similar, because both processes entail reflection and sharing and both are geared to support the development of a clearer understanding of oneself, particularly as this pertains to interactions in a life-world or a system-world context. Sharing as co-creation (to use Hunt's terminology) is one of a number of powerful ways in which communicative action can occur.

Process Stages

The fundamental assumptions of renewal are that we possess a reservoir of ideas, are creative and are capable of drawing from our own experience what will sustain us in our further renewal journey. Without confidence in the self, a readiness to explore options and a reflective approach, it is unlikely that our renewal experiences will succeed. These basic needs can be built upon with appropriate techniques to initiate transformation.

A cycle of renewal may typically include the following interrelated stages:

C	Concern	"What we are concerned about?"
Re	Reflection	"What have we got?"
A	Action	"What can we do?"
T	Try out	"Doing what we set out to do."
E	Evaluate	"What are the outcomes and have we improved the situation?"

The cycle is used to develop an action plan. This can be done individually or, as mentioned earlier in the discussion on sharing images, is ideally undertaken with a partner or a group of peers. The degree to which the process cycle is used successfully and collaboratively will usually depend on the degree of trust in the group and the nature of the concern (e.g., personal or professional).

It can be helpful to document your renewal activities by means of a personal mission statement. This would emerge after the C-Re-A-T-E cycle has been applied and represent what is achievable and yet also be a challenge. Your mission statement should therefore be clear and purposeful. It should specify direction and provide aims. It can act as a measure from which your future behaviours can be evaluated and, above all, should be personalised. In other words, unless it possesses real meaning for your personal activities it will have a limited chance of being used. It should be simple, able to be committed to memory and reviewed daily. It should act as the basis for all other activities and be life-giving.

Management Principles

What becomes critical for the co-creation strategy is the quality of the interpersonal relationships between the individuals involved, and basic principles for keeping on track. Feeling goodwill, having respect for self and respect for the non-disclosure of some information, being non-judgemental about personal reactions, possessing an openness to feelings and a willingness to trust yourself and the other person are central to the process.

Principles that will assist with the overall management of renewal should be determined. These will vary in accordance with the individual or organisation concerned, but may include such things as recognising incremental growth, working on achievable outcomes, providing rewards, celebrating achievements, being mindful of collaboration, integrating system- and life-world needs and so on. These principles will serve to keep you or a group on task so that renewal can be built on values.

REFLECtION 8.2

What principles and processes of renewal would have the greatest impact on your personal renewal? Why are those you have chosen so important?

Personal Renewal

Personal renewal begins with identifying what you believe is important for self-development. This may range from a particular ambition (e.g., a qualification, a position at work), a religious conviction or simply be an attempt to balance your life by a healthy combination of satisfying experiences. If it is important enough, then seeking an image that visualises what you value, identifying a concrete symbol to bring this to mind and finally undertaking behaviours that actually typify your value in operation are the next steps. Table 8.1 is offered as a guide to this process.

Moving from reflections to documenting ideas provides a basis for commitment and clarification and can act as a check on action taken or merely reflected on. The notion of imageing and symbolising is to give reinforcement, while typical behaviours will help illustrate practical application of the value.

An example of personal renewal might be to select as a value the notion of balance in life; that is, opportunities should exist for a variety of interests (family, work, hobbies, sports, etc.). An image that might typify this is the *image* of a home within which there are occasions for all of these activities. The home might allow for gardening, family time, sports and occasions for reflection. The *symbol* could be pictures of individual activities or perhaps a composite collection such as a photographic collage. *Behaviours* associated with the value would include providing for family time, recreation, work and meditative experiences.

Interpersonal Renewal

The notion of linking values, image, symbol and behaviour would also apply to interpersonal functioning. In the area of relationships it is possible to identify a value or values that would underpin how you would want to relate to others and

Table 8.1
Guide to Personal Renewal

Value/s:
Images:
Symbols:
Typical Behaviours:

the image, symbol and behaviour that would characterise this. Values applicable to this domain could be trust, service, respect, faithfulness and honesty. An image of the interpersonal value of service may be that of waiting on tables, while a symbol could be an appropriate item of apparel. Behaviours typical of service might include preparedness to help, putting others first, helping without being prompted, being sensitive and so on.

Managerial Renewal

Management entails the practice of stewardship over personal resources and, in the case of a position of responsibility, oversight of the outputs of particular individuals. Values associated with this area could include efficiency, development, prudence, rationality and empowerment. An image for the value of empowerment might be that of the horticulturalist who cares professionally and carefully for all plants within the garden. A symbol could be a piece of equipment, while behaviours would be nurturing, monitoring, planting ideas and providing an appropriate environment for growth.

Organisational Renewal

Thriving in organisations is dependent on understanding one's position, the structures and systems that comprise the business and being aware of the culture that prevails. Values that meet an individual's appreciation of this might be knowledge, communication and alignment. An image for alignment could be a tree with varying branches that are linked, connected, interdependent and symmetrical, while a symbol may represent some or all of this image (e.g., a branch, piece of bark or leaf collage). Behaviours that reflect that the person is operating with these values in mind might include understanding organisational goals, being available, exercising regular communication, being cooperative, sharing resources and showing interest.

APPLICATION

Sharing Images
The significance of the *image* as a basis for sharing ideas rests in its power to capture the message in the exchange. The overall process is relatively straightforward and is comprised of the following phases:
1. Phase One — image identification
- Personal reflection on image/s to be shared (performed alone)
- Selection of a partner to share image/s with.

2. Phase Two — image sharing
- First person immerses themselves in the image and describes feelings, sensations, features, etc.
- Partner listens and paraphrases the experience, and provides a "mirror" for it.

Conclusion

The concept of renewal provides a framework for integrating much of the material presented in this text. A commitment to renewal will permit reflection on content and an opportunity for practical application of the ideas presented. Renewal is more than mere change. It is based on drawing meaning from activities and experiences and examining how development can occur in personal, interpersonal, managerial and organisational aspects of life.

Renewal is concerned with personal transformation that balances the significance of subjective (life-world) and objective (system-world) pressures. It can be reflected on and supported by the use of images and symbols, which can be enhanced when shared with others and is most fully realised when behaviours are lived out. It is assisted by capturing elements within a mission statement that characterises a commitment to renewal and provides a means for review of actions deemed appropriate.

Chapter 8
Keeping on, Keeping on: Sustaining Interpersonal Development Through Renewal

People skills are at the heart of renewal. They trigger and facilitate action and are themselves the recipient of effort and outcomes.

Chapter 9
Putting It All Together

The motivation for this text came from a desire to piece together a little of the extensive literature on people skills. In drafting our ideas we were constantly reminded that the destination of the journey (interpersonal development) was not to be the only goal. In other words, by living life fully, with open eyes, a clear head and with hands willing to take up challenges, the excitement and rewards of "travel" would be there in abundance. To become interpersonally effective at the end of the journey may be the goal, but to try and be interpersonally effective as one lives out the journey is more worthwhile. We hope, therefore, that the material of this text does encourage exploration and that through "being" and "doing" you do "find" some solutions, joys and growth.

The pattern of growth in people skills will vary for everyone. There is no one model. Rather, your approach is premised on the personal values that you believe are integral and appropriate. The challenge is therefore yours. It is to be reflective and renewing and in so doing to begin with yourself and thereby provide a foundation for development in other domains of personal functioning. It is about recognising the connections within your own being, the connections that exist with others and the knowledge that in all of this there are people skills that support and develop from your engagement and reflection.

Connection within the domains of our personal being (cognition, affect, physical, social, spiritual) and connection across social environments (relationships, groups, family, workplace) suggests that activity in any one area is never independent of another. The ecology of the person within the broader ecology of life allows for multiple opportunities for intervention and development. People skills are at the heart of this life-long journey.

We wish you well in your continuing growth with interpersonal development and trust that something of our journey may be helpful to your own people skills.

APPLICATION

Think about this situation that another person is experiencing and try to address a process that might be used to deal with this. Review your readings from each chapter in considering your responses.

John was an only child who was brought up in a rigid and strict home environment. His father was a dominant person who was authoritarian and lacked compassion. John's mother was very caring and even protective but had no real authority in the home. John was lonely as a child and never really learnt to relate easily to others. He was a high achiever academically and at sport, but tended to be an anxious person.

John's friendships tended to be with marginalised students and these social patterns continued at university. When he began work he was still somewhat of a loner and was regularly in conflict situations with other staff. When John was promoted he became a benevolent dictator who responded well to the needs of staff as long as they accepted his authority. He was not a leader to cross.

When working in groups John appeared to be a good listener and a collaborative worker, but in fact got his agenda through with very little adjustment. He was creative in the organisation but very demanding on staff in terms of performance. People liked the challenge of working with him but found it stressful.

- What are the major features of this individual that might impact upon his interpersonal development?
- What suggestions would you make about how to improve his view of himself and his ability to work with others?
- Working in groups and within organisations requires skills and sensitivity. What could John do to enhance his effectiveness within these settings?
- As a leader what are his strengths and weaknesses and how could he best build upon them?

Try to incorporate all aspects of the person in constructing these responses. You are really assisting someone to develop and refine their people skills as a pathway to interpersonal development.

Bibliography

Belbin, R.M. (1981) *Management teams: Why they succeed or fail.* London, Heinemann.

Beck, A. (1988). *Love is not enough.* NY: Harper Row.

Bennis, W., & Nanus, B. (1985). *Leader strategies for taking charge.* New York: Harper Row.

Bredeson, P.V. (1988). Perspectives on schools: metaphors and management in education. *The Journal of Educational Administration, 26,* 293–310.

Corwin, R.G. (1987). Models of educational organizations. *Review of Research in Education, 2,* 247–295.

Carew, D.K., Parisi-Carew, E., & Blanchard, K.H. (1986). Group development and situational leadership: A model for managing groups. *Training and Development Journal, June,* 46–50.

Crowther, F. (1999). *Parallel leadership.* Address, Annual General Meeting, Australian College of Education, Darling Downs Chapter.

Crowther, F. (2001). *The teaching profession: The dawn of a new era.* G.W. Bassett Memorial Oration,Brisbane, Australian College of Education, Queensland Chapter.

Duignan, P. (1987). Leaders as culture builders. *Unicorn, 13,* 208–213.

Ellis, A. (2002). *Coping with the suicide of a loved one* [videotape]. New York: Institute for Rational-Emotive Therapy.

Fisher, R., & Ury, W. (1997). *Getting to yes.* Melbourne: Business Books.

Habermas, J. (1984a). *The theory of communicative action: The reason and rationalisation of society: Volume 1.* Boston, USA: Beacon Press.

Habermas, J. (1984b). *The theory of communicative action: The critique of functionalist reason: Volume 2.* Boston, USA: Beacon Press.

Hersey, P., & Blanchard, K.H. (1977). *Management of organizational behaviour* (3rd ed.). New Jersey: Prentice-Hall.

Hunt, D.E. (1987). *Beginning with ourselves.* Cambridge, Ma: Brookline.

Hunt, D.E. (1991). *The renewal of personal energy.* Ontario: OISE Press.

Johnson, D.W. (1987). *Reaching out: Interpersonal development and Self actualisation* (3rd ed.). New Jersey: Prentice Hall.

Luft, J. (1969). *Of human interaction.* Palo Alto, California: National Press Books.

McKinney, M.B. (1987). *Sharing wisdom.* Chicago: Falcon Publications.

Morgan, G. (1986). *Images of organization.* Beverley Hills: Sage Publications.

Okun, B. (1987) *Effective helping: Interviewing and counselling techniques.* North Scituate, Mass: Duxbury Press.

Robbins, S.P., Waters-Marsh, T., Cacioppe, R., & Millett, B. (1994). *Organisational behaviour: Concepts, controversies and applications.* New York: Prentice Hall.

Ryan, E.R., Hawkins, M., & Russell, R. (1992). Education: An exchange of ideas among three humanistic psychologists. *Journal of Humanistic Education and Development 30,* 178–191.

Schein, E.H. (1985). *Organizational culture and leadership: A dynamic view.* San Francisco: Jossey-Bass.

Sergiovanni, T.J. (1987). *The Principalship: A reflective practice perspective.* Massachusetts: Allyn & Bacon.

Spry, V.G., Sultmann, W.F., & Ralston, F.M. (1992). Imageing: shared meaning for curriculum renewal and school development. *Issues in Education No. 6.* Brisbane: Ministerial Consultative Council on Curriculum.

Tannenbaum, R., Weschler, I., & Massarik, F. (1961). *Leadership and organisation.* New York: McGraw Hill.

Timm, P.R., Peterson, D.D., & Stevens, J.C. (1990). *People at work: Human relations in organizations* (3rd ed.). Minneapolis: West Publishing Co St Paul.

Trotzer, J.P. (1989). *The counsellor and the group: Integrating theory, training and practice.* Muncie, Indiana: Accelerated Development Inc.

Tuckman, B. (1965). Developmental sequence in small groups. *Psychological Bulletin, 63,* 381–399.

Verderber, R.F., & Verderber, K.S. (1989). *Beginnings in relational communication.* New York: John Wiley & Sons.

Wheatley, M. (1992). *Leadership and the new science: learning about organizations from an orderly universe.* San Francisco: Berrett-Koehler Publishers.

Wheatley, M., & Kellner-Rogers, M. (1996). *A simpler way.* San Francisco: Berrett-Koehler.

PEOPLE SKILLS guiding you to effective interpersonal behaviour

www.ingramcontent.com/pod-product-compliance
Lightning Source LLC
Chambersburg PA
CBHW071850230426
43671CB00012B/2136